THE
CATHEDRAL
CAT

THE CATHEDRAL CAT

STORIES FROM EXETER CATHEDRAL

Nicholas Orme

IMPRESS BOOKS

First published October 2008
Reprinted November 2008
by Impress Books Ltd
Innovation Centre, Rennes Drive,
University of Exeter Campus, Exeter EX4 4RN

Typeset in 10/13 Palatino by Swales and Willis Ltd, Exeter, Devon

Printed and bound in England by imprint-academic.com

British Library Cataloguing in Publication Data
A catalogue record for this book is available from the British Library

ISBN: 978 0 9556239 4 3

In memory of Bruce McFarlane, medieval historian, and his cats:
Hodge, The Lord Edward, Abelard and Origen,
Bogo de Clare, and Jasper Tudor

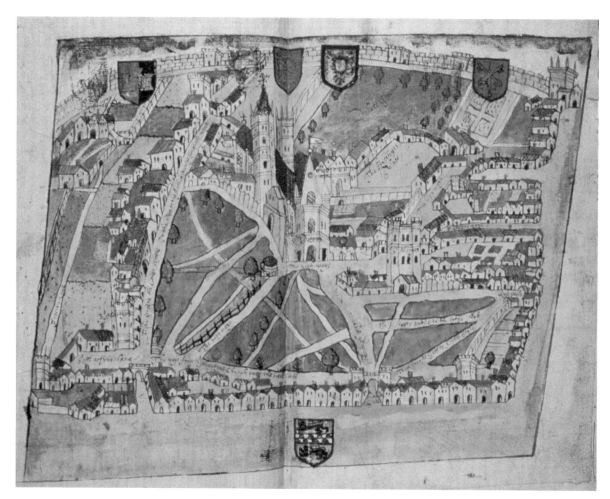

Exeter Cathedral and its close in the late sixteenth century

CONTENTS

PREFACE

Most of the chapters of this book appeared as short articles in the *Annual Report of the Friends of Exeter Cathedral* between 1981 and 2003. I have revised them and added four others to make a group of sixteen. The stories relate to places and objects that can still be seen in and around Exeter Cathedral, or in its library and archives, and I hope that they will give pleasure to those who visit the building and study its history. Two other pieces by me in the *Annual Report*, on the Anglo-Saxon minster at Exeter and the records of Mortehoe parish, are not reproduced here because they fit less well into this anthology.

I am grateful to the Friends for allowing me to reprint the articles, Julie Willis for taking the photographs, the dean and chapter for permission to reproduce them, John Allan for his long-standing advice and encouragement, the cathedral librarians and archivists for their support over several decades, and my publishers, Impress Books, for their kindness in enabling this book to appear.

Nicholas Orme,
Oxford,
2008

1 GOING BACK: FEBRUARY 1385

And there the bells are ringing
In heaven's court afar:
Oh that we were there!
Oh that we were there!
Carol: In Dulci Jubilo

I am standing in deep shadow under an archway, beneath a high building. Dawn has not yet broken, and the darkness around me is lightened only by gleams behind the shutters of the houses opposite, glinting on the puddles in the street. Within the archway are two massive wooden gates, damp from the winter night, before which I am standing. I am not alone. I can sense rather than see that there are three or four others beside me, and I can hear footsteps approaching: a man's boots, slow and heavy, and the lighter quicker sound of a woman's shoes. Now there are six or seven of us waiting beside the gates.

Suddenly the silence is broken by the sound of a bell in the distance, thin and mellow. It is Clerematin, ringing high up in the south tower. There is a noise behind the gates. A key grates in a lock. Bolts are drawn back. A door opens in one of the gates, revealing a dim hooded figure. I cannot see him clearly but I know who he is: Richard Scot, priest of the Bitton chantry and porter of the close.[1]

Other churches have laymen porters. This cathedral has a priest. Ever since the precentor was murdered and gates were put round the cathedral close, one of the clergy has locked them at dusk and opened them at dawn to ensure the safety of his brothers. Not that Sir Richard is as careful as he should be. There have been complaints in the mayor's court that he leaves the gates open after curfew, letting men in and out against the peace.[2] This is the treasurer's fault. He neglects to keep the close in good order, and the lesser clergy take their lead from him.[3]

We pass in turn through the door and walk under the arches of the Broad Gate. The bell continues to ring. As I emerge from the gate, the night sky is beginning to lighten above the huge black shapes of the buildings below it. My shoes squelch on the wet and muddy road. On my right, I can make out the big tower and the north walls of the church of St Mary Major. Beside it, but much smaller, is the dim outline of the charnel chapel. As I go past it I think of the charnel beneath the chapel where the bones are stacked by the pitmaker, the bones he turns up when he digs new graves in the close.[4] *Requiem eternam dona eis, Domine, et lux perpetua luceat eis.*

Now the cathedral looms before us, and we turn to the left, past the north-west corner and along the north side of the building. The cathedral entrance, for which we are making, is not one of the doors in the west front. They are used only for processions of clergy or by important visitors like King Richard, who went through the great west door when he came here as a boy with his mother. We enter, as people normally do, through the north porch. We pass the statue of Our Lady in the porch with its collecting box – *Ave Maria plena gracia* – and come beneath the gaze of the two small windows through which the custors (sacristans) keep watch on the porch. They are not watching now, because it is a lawful time to come in and the north door has been unlocked. The foremost of us turns the ring and opens it, and we file down the steps to the nave, disturbing a cat which slips into the shadows.

Clerematin grows fainter as we enter. There are other sounds: coughing, soft footfalls of leather soles and sharper noises from doors or small gates. The cathedral is dim rather than dark, revealing the piers of the nave rising up to the vaulting and the outlines of the screen in front of the choir. Two lights burn on the parapet of the screen, so that the image of Christ on the Cross above them appears in a dramatic contrast of light and shadow. Below the screen are the two nave altars, each surrounded by railings of wood and metal. The altar on the left side – Our Lady in the Nave, also known as the Bratton chantry – has its candles lit ready for mass, the mass for which we have come.

Steps are now heard approaching in the south choir aisle. The aisle door opens, and two figures emerge from it. In front I recognise Robert Lyngham, one of the young men known as secondaries who sit in the second row of the choir. He is the clerk on duty for this mass, in cassock and surplice.[5] Behind him comes Sir William Bonok, the priest of the Bratton chantry who celebrates mass at this altar every day. He is wearing vestments: chasuble, stole, and maniple.[6] Bonok is Cornish – one of a few such men on the staff, since the cathedral is the mother church of Cornwall as well as Devon. Once there were three priests of the Bratton chantry, but since the Black Death there have been only two, and one of the posts is vacant, so a vicar choral is paid to act as the second Bratton priest.

The Bratton altar is important because the first masses of the day are said here at dawn – 'morrow' (morning) masses as they are called. Bonok will say his first, and when he has finished his colleague priest will say another. The cathedral has eighteen altars where masses are said each day, and all the chantry priests (known here as annuellars) say one of these masses, as do several of the vicars choral. But no other mass may be said until the Bratton masses are over, so the other clergy can sleep for a little longer before they come in for their duties. The close gates and cathedral doors are opened at dawn to let pious local people attend the masses before they start work. That is why our little group is here.

The clerk opens the gate in the railings around the altar, goes in, and holds the gate aside for Sir William. Then he closes it, reminding us that the priest and his clerk will say mass, and Jesus will make his bodily appearance in bread and wine, in a holy secluded space. We stay outside: allowed to watch and pray, but not expected to say anything. Sir William will celebrate the mass, and Lyngham will read the epistle and make the responses. We may do what we like, as long as we are not noisy or irreverent.

Sir William starts to read aloud from his missal. He reads quickly in his Cornish accent, *Deus cui omne cor patet et omnis voluntas loquitur, et quem nullum latet secretum* . . . We gather round the screens beside the altar: standing, leaning, or kneeling. One man has brought a book of hours and is reading it aloud to himself. It is not the same book as Sir William's missal, for only a few wealthy lay people bring their own missals to follow the service in church. Books of hours contain more simple Latin prayers, and people buy them to have something devout to read at service times.

The rest of us have our rosaries, and we say the Latin *Ave Maria* in tens, with a *Paternoster* (Lord's Prayer) after each set of ten, keeping track of what we are doing by running the beads through our fingers. Most people's rosaries are made of wooden beads, but if you came to the ten o'clock mass that is popular with the merchants' wives, you would see ones of silver, coral, or even gold.

Still, as we finger our beads we do not ignore the mass altogether, and we know when the climax approaches because Sir William drops his voice and mutters the prayer of consecration to himself. *Te igitur clementissime pater per Jesum Christum filium tuum* . . . Then he holds up the consecrated wafer and the chalice while we kneel and doff our hoods or hats in reverence. Christ is here before us in the form of the bread and wine.

In his presence, the priest commends to him the souls of Henry de Bratton and Sir John Wyger, who endowed this chantry mass. Then he takes the ivory disc called the pax, kisses it, and passes it to the secondary. Lyngham kisses it and brings it out to us, and we kiss it in turn. Meanwhile the priest consumes the wafer and drinks the wine from the chalice.

The mass now speeds to its end. *In nomine patris et filii et spiritus sancti. Amen.* Already the next priest is approaching: Sir John Govys.[7] Sir William bows to the altar, and the gate in the railings is opened. He passes out and his colleague goes in, while Lyngham remains to perform his duties all over again. The bystanders break up. People walk back to the north door thinking of breakfast and their work. The second mass begins, and I am now the only observer apart from the cat, which has reappeared. The worship of the cathedral goes on irrespective of whether lay people are present or not.

By the time the second mass is over, the cathedral is coming to life. Two bells are ringing to call the clergy to prime – the first service of the day. Some walk in through the north door, while others appear from an entrance on the south side. Lights have been lit in the choir. The clergy who are coming in wear surplices over black cassocks. They are alone or in pairs, not attended by servants. That means they are not canons, who are too grand to come to prime. These are the minor clergy, the workhorses of the cathedral: adult vicars choral and annuellars and teenage secondaries, about forty of them altogether. There is also a small group of choristers – not all of them, but only those who are needed. The rest are learning music in the song school opposite the west front of the cathedral. As each person enters the choir, the cleric on duty (the punctator) stands by the choir door with his list of names and pricks each one. Later, the list will be inspected, and if anyone is missing without a good reason, he will be hauled before the chapter and fined.

I would weary you if I tried to tell more of the day. But I hope I have shown you what I love about the cathedral: its ability to take us back to its past. When I see the stones of the building and their decorations, I think of the masons and limners who worked them hundreds of years ago. I can find where they got their stones and materials. When I work in the archives, I can read the very handwriting of the clerks of the exchequer, the clerk of the works, and the collectors of rents in the city. I can learn the names of many canons, vicars, annuellars, and secondaries – everyone but the choristers – and even those of the workmen, when they worked, and what they were paid. So much has survived of the cathedral's past that you may constantly return to it, as I have done here, and glimpse its people and what they did, as if they were still alive.

2 THE CATHEDRAL CAT

I and Pangur Ban my cat,
'Tis a like thing we are at.
Hunting mice is his delight;
Hunting words I sit all night.
Medieval Irish Lyric

Every cathedral has a cat in it, and this is probably almost as true of cathedrals during their history as it is of their spelling. As long as there have been large churches, they have suffered invasions from rats and mice on the ground levels and birds in the upper storeys, and their human guardians have needed the help of cats to keep the invaders at bay. There was a cat at the abbey of Bec in Normandy as early as the 1040s, when Lanfranc was a monk there and took the cat away with him, wrapped in a cloth and mewing loudly, to help catch vermin on one of the abbey estates for which he was responsible.[1] Records of church cats in medieval England are difficult to find, however, and a special interest therefore attaches to the discovery of references to the cat of Exeter Cathedral during the fourteenth and fifteenth centuries. The references become even more intriguing when we learn not merely that a cat existed, but that it held a recognised position as a member of the cathedral staff, with a regular salary!

'This is the cat that killed the rat.' The carving of one-eyed Tom in the chapel of St James

The officer in charge of the cathedral interior and its furnishings, in medieval times, was the treasurer, one of the canons. In practice, the day-to-day care of the building was deputed to the four custors who acted as the virgers do today: ringing for services, keeping visitors in order, and looking after the vestments. The treasurer was entitled to half the money from the collecting boxes in the cathedral, out of which he had to pay fees to the custors, the grave-digger, the seamstress, the laundress, and the cat. The records of these transactions are to be found in the obit accounts, which survive from 1305 until 1467.[2] For nearly the whole of this period they include a regular payment of 13*d.* each quarter of the year 'to the custors and the cat' (*custoribus et cato*). The exception consists of the accounts between Christmas 1363 and Michaelmas 1366 when, for a brief period, the payment was doubled to 26*d.*[3] It is possible that this reflects the appointment of a second cat to the staff. The word 'cats' in the plural (*catis*) certainly appears once, in the account for Easter 1378, indicating that there were sometimes more than one.[4] We do not know when the payment ceased to be made. It is noted as late as about 1547, in a paper record of cathedral accounts, but is there said to be for the *custoribus* only.[5]

The evidence of the obit accounts shows that the cat was a junior adjutant to the custors. How much of the payment of 13*d.* was passed on to the cat itself is never directly stated, but the records throw a gleam of light on the question. In 1384 the treasurer, Robert Broke, protested to the archbishop of Canterbury about certain moneys which, he claimed, were being unlawfully withheld from him by the cathedral chapter – the whole body of canons. At the same time, he complained, he was still expected to bear his accustomed financial burdens, including an annual payment of 4s. 4d. 'for the cat' (*pro cato*).[6] The chapter, in their answer, tried to make fun of this particular point by referring to the cat as a little one (*catulo*).[7] Nevertheless, the treasurer's use of the phrase 'for the cat' is copied by some of the obit accounts, which occasionally substitute it for the usual formula 'and the cat'. This suggests that the whole sum was indeed intended for the cat's benefit. Thirteen pence a quarter, or 4s. 4d. a year, is exactly a penny a week. The cat would have been required to be partially self-supporting, in order to keep down the birds and rodents, but no respectable cat expects to feed itself entirely, and no doubt the weekly penny was spent on cat's-meat for its dinners, as a due reward for its services.

The rat that Tom caught – also in St James's chapel

It is unfortunate, given the cat's contribution to cathedral life, that it was never commemorated by a medieval carving when the building was being beautified. The earliest archaeological evidence about the cat, which is still to be seen today, is the cat-hole in the door in the north wall of the north transept, beneath the clock, which enabled the cat to extend its rounds up the staircase inside. Happily, the lack of a medieval representation was remedied when the chapel of St James was rebuilt after the Second World War. A fine cat's head, with only one eye, may now be observed in the north-west corner, on the right hand as you enter. This is a memorial to Tom, the cat of the head virger, Mr E. R. Hart, during and after the war. Tom lost his eye in a fight with an owl for a rat, which is represented on a corbel in the opposite north-east

corner of the chapel.[8] He looks fierce on his carving, but one lady who attended the cathedral as a girl in the 1930s said that he liked people and would come and sit on the seat beside her.[9]

The dean and chapter no longer employ a cat officially, although one or two may often be seen about the cathedral precincts. These, like Tom, belong to members of the cathedral staff or else they are interlopers: secular cats from the world beyond the close. The true 'cathedral cat' lives only in the archives.

The cat hole through the tower door in the north transept

3 A SPOON FOR EVERY VICAR

> You may have my rich brocades, my laces; take each household key;
> Ransack coffer, chest, bureau;
> Quiz the few poor treasures hid there, con the letters kept by me.
> *Thomas Hardy, 'Friends Beyond'*

'Where there's a will there's a way.' Few documents reveal the past more vividly. Wills are pieces of autobiography, often the only ones that survive about the people who made them. They reflect their makers' beliefs and concerns. They often cast light on families and friends. Frequently they tell us about the social conditions in which their makers lived, including their property, lifestyle, and surroundings. The oldest surviving will of one of Exeter's cathedral clergy is that of Thomas Boteler, archdeacon of Totnes, made in 1263. Unfortunately it says little about the cathedral.[1] The next is that of Henry de Berbilond, one of the vicars choral, dating from 1296. This turned up in a sale of documents at Sothebys in 1992 and was bought for the cathedral archives with the help of the Friends of Exeter Cathedral and a grant from the Museums and Galleries Commission.[2] Henry's will is all one could desire. It goes into minute detail about his possessions, and specified what was to happen to them in some eighty-eight different bequests. It also gives us valuable information about the cathedral and its community.[3]

What was a vicar choral? Answering this question involves explaining the staffing of a medieval cathedral like Exeter. The cathedral was run by twenty-four canons, not all of whom were resident. Four of the canons – the dean, precentor, chancellor, and treasurer – had specific responsibilities, but all the canons were equal 'in chapter' at their meetings. When Bishop Leofric founded the cathedral in 1050, the canons were expected to say the daily services, but by the thirteenth century they had become too important to do this work, which involved being present in church at intervals from the early hours of the morning up to the late afternoon. Accordingly, each canon appointed a deputy to act in his place – a vicar choral. The vicars turned up to every service, and the canons put in an appearance at one or two. Eventually there were other clergy – between eighteen and twenty-one chantry priests, known as 'annuellars'; twelve teenage or young adult clerks called 'secondaries'; and fourteen choristers. In all, the cathedral staff numbered some seventy or eighty souls, up to the Reformation.[4]

The canons were relatively well paid, with daily allowances and shares in the income of the cathedral. The vicars, being lowlier, earned less, but they were adequately rewarded by the standards of the day. They each got their meals with their canon and possibly slept in his house. Eventually, after 1382, they lived in a street of little houses in Kalendarhay. They were paid from a mixture of sources including £1 from the cathedral, a share of the income of Woodbury church which was given to them jointly by Bishop Henry Marshal, and various other allowances. In Berbilond's time, round about 1300, a vicar could probably expect to receive around £3 a year in cash, with perks worth a further pound or two from living with his canon. This was more than a chantry priest or curate was paid, and approached the stipends of the clergy of the less wealthy parish churches. It helped to determine the social class from which the vicars came. Canons were usually sons of the gentry or of wealthy citizens of Exeter. Vicars' fathers would have been prosperous farmers (the kinds of people later known as 'yeomen') or else craftsmen or shopkeepers.

What we know of Henry de Berbilond's origins fits well with this model. He seems to have originated from Silverton, a few miles north of Exeter, since his will includes bequests to its church and to people in its parish. His surname, 'of Berbilond', probably came from a farm a mile south of the village, nowadays known as Babylon. He may have been born there. Socially, he seems to have belonged to a well-to-do family on the land. One of his nephews had the non-aristocratic name of William Podyng and another was a smith, but William Podyng had married into the Sechevills, a minor gentry family who held the manor of Combe (or Culm) Sechevill in Silverton. This suggests that Henry was below the gentry in rank but not very far below. For such a man, a post as a vicar choral had similar status and wealth to that of his family, carrying as it did a reasonable income and the possibility of rising higher. The dean and chapter chose the clergy of a good many parish churches in Devon and Cornwall, and they often promoted dutiful vicars to these churches, giving them larger incomes than they received at the cathedral.

The stair to the custors' room above the north porch. The rail allowed them to feel their way down in the dark

We know much less about the vicars of Henry's day than we do a hundred or two hundred years later. Even their names have largely perished before 1300. In Henry's case, it is thought that he was a vicar by 1282 and that he continued to be one until he died, probably on 17 October 1296. The mention in his will of some grown-up nephews suggests that he was then a man of at least fifty, who had been born some years before the middle of the thirteenth century. The will was drawn up on 8 October, shortly before his death, when he foresaw his approaching end. By this time he owned a good deal of goods and property, as much or almost as much as a canon. He had a house of his own in the cathedral close, so he did not need to live with the canon for whom he deputised. Outside Exeter he held a lease of land at Landscore and Ratsloe in Poltimore parish, where he had farm servants working for him. He

A misericord, a shelf for resting the bottom of a vicar choral as he stood in the choir

also owned a field in Budleigh Salterton. He seems to have been the steward or supervisor of the vicars' property at Woodbury, and must have been privileged to miss some of the cathedral services, since he had access to a house at Woodbury, sometimes spent the night there, and talks of 'his' reeve, who was probably the vicars' local agent in the parish.

His Exeter house stood on the north-west side of the close, in the block that backs on to the High Street. According to his will, it contained 'a best bed in which I lie', wall hangings, brass pots, wooden cups and dishes, a chest that could be locked, and linen including towels and tablecloths. His clothes included a gown, tabards, and surcoats in the clerical colours of black or white, some of which were decorated with fur. He also had surplices and mass vestments of his own for cathedral services. One of his best possessions was a maple wood cup with a silver base, which he gave in his will to the dean of Exeter, and he had enough silver spoons to leave one to each of his twenty-three fellow vicars. This last bequest is particularly useful for cathedral history, because it adds a number of their names to those we know. Another valuable item was a rosary whose beads were made of coral: he gave it to Woodbury church. He had at least one servant, a man as would be expected in a clergyman's house, but a laundress came in to deal with his washing. Her name was Margaret, and he left her two wall hangings and two sheets.

When you made a will in the middle ages, there was an accepted form in which you, or the literate person you employed, wrote it down. You began by bequeathing your soul to God and then you made your funeral arrangements. Henry bequeathed £10 for his funeral, a large sum equal to at least two years' salary for a vicar choral. He wanted this money to be used to pay for the funeral service (it was customary to make a substantial offering at the funeral mass), for candles to burn around his corpse before and during the service, and for a distribution of money to the poor. He asked to be buried in a worn set of priest's vestments. He did not state where all this should happen, but he is likely to have died at his house in the cathedral close, to have had his funeral in the cathedral, and to have been buried in the cathedral cemetery – now the cathedral green – as were most people in Exeter.

After making the funeral arrangements, a will would list charitable bequests. Henry gave sums of money to the two Exeter friaries, because friars depended on voluntary donations. He also remembered the poor sick people who lived in the hospital of St John in the High Street, the lepers in their hospital in Magdalen Road, and the prisoners in Exeter gaol. Gifts like these are common in Exeter wills, and people would have been expected to make them. Henry's chief bequest was to give his Exeter house to the vicars choral in perpetuity. They would have rented the house to a tenant, and he intended them to use part of the rent to finance two masses a year for ever, with payments to the cathedral clergy who attended them. One mass was to be said for his soul and the other for the soul of a former canon, Gilbert de Tytinges, who seems to have been Henry's patron and possibly his relative.

With the charities disposed of, a will-maker could go on to make bequests to his family and friends. Henry seems to have had no brother or sister alive, but he had an aunt named Clara to whom he gave some clothes and bedclothes, and several nephews. One of these was given his country estate at Landscore. This was evidently a flourishing concern, since it came with six oxen, six bullocks, twenty sheep, carts, a waggon, and farm implements. His godchildren got 6d. each, not a large sum but one that is paralleled in other wills and suggests that medieval godparents were not necessarily closer to their godchildren than they are in modern times. He was more generous to some other young people. One youth got £2 'that he may be instructed in some craft', and three groups of children received 10s., 4s., and 2s. to share among them. There must have been great interest in the disposition of Henry's property when he died, and no doubt some were pleased with their windfalls and others unhappy.

Sometimes we can get a sense from wills of what their makers were like. I see Henry as a practical man, a good administrator. He was able to combine his work as a vicar choral with duties at Woodbury and the management of a farm at Poltimore. He was the guardian of one his nephews who was still a child, and of the nephew's property. Several of his bequests were useful ones. He gave some timber that he owned to make a new door for the vicars' grange at Woodbury, and he left sums of money for the upkeep of six local bridges. Four of these are well-known structures – at Bishop's Clyst, Exeter, Stoke Canon, and Thorverton. The fifth bridge, 'on the other side of the Creedy towards the house of Sir Herbert', is identifiable as Pynes Bridge leading to Pynes and Upton Pyne, the former property of Sir Herbert de Pyne. The sixth, described as *Hederdyg* (which means 'deer-fence' or 'ha-ha'), must be Ellerhayes Bridge, which carries the road from Silverton to Broadclyst across the River Culm. It lies close by the deer-fence boundary to the north of Killerton House. Until 1816 a branch of the main road from Exeter to Taunton and Bristol passed that way.

One can imagine Henry riding across these bridges on his journeys from Exeter out to his property at Silverton or to other places, keeping a sharp eye on their condition, and feeling that he should do his bit towards repairing them. He did – and all six bridges are still with us. In such ways, wills can give us glimpses beyond people's deathbeds and tell us things about their active lives.

4 WHOSE BODY?

> In charnel at church, churls are hard to know,
> Or a knight from a knave, or a quean from a queen.
> *William Langland, Piers Plowman*

A popular legend of the middle ages, often retold in writings and pictured in art, was the story of 'The Three Living and the Three Dead'. Three young men are enjoying themselves out hunting when they are horrified by the appearance of three ghastly shapes in the form of decaying corpses. The living ask the dead who they are. The dead reply 'Yourselves! We were once like you, and you will become like us when you are rotting in the ground.'

There are three mysterious bodies in the cathedral, mysterious because they have no inscriptions to say who they were. Two are effigies of knights and the third is that of a corpse. The knights are to be found side by side in the south choir aisle, 'crusader knights' as such figures are often called, although both these date from about the first thirty years of the fourteenth century when crusading was not very common. A more accurate description would be 'effigies in the vigorous artistic style of the thirteenth and early fourteenth centuries'. Each knight lies under an arched recess within the choir wall. The recess on the right has a flattened ogival arch, richly carved with foliage, which looks contemporary with its effigy. The one on the left has a plain arch and was evidently inserted later, because it cuts slightly into its right-hand neighbour. Its back wall shows signs of renewal, but this is a result of the bombing of the cathedral in 1942.

In the sixteenth and early seventeenth centuries, the knights' shields were apparently still painted with coats of arms, and the identities that have been attributed to them are based on that evidence. Since 1542 the knight on the left has been regarded as a member of a Devonshire family, either Ralegh or Chichester, and by a generation or two later his neighbour on the right was considered to be Humphrey de Bohun III, earl of Hereford and Essex, who died in 1322. These attributions have often been repeated, but although they have given rise to discussion they have generally been accepted, and this account is the first to challenge them.

The earliest mention of the knights occurs in the notes of John Leland, who visited the cathedral in 1542. He recorded in Latin, 'in the south choir aisle . . . Chichester, knight'.[1] He is silent about the other tomb, and although a silence is a weaker basis for an argument than a fact, I am inclined to think that its identity was not clear or known at this time, since Leland walked along the south choir aisle (where he noted the Oldham chapel) and busied himself in recording the major tombs. The next witness is Sir George Carew, who produced a guide to the heraldry of Devon in 1588. He does not identify the knights' positions, but he gives descriptions of two coats of arms that could well relate to them:

> B[lue] bet[ween] a bend ar[gent] 2 cotizes or, bet[ween] 6 lions rampant or, 3 (3). Bohun, Earle of Hereford and Essex, he lieth buried in St Peter's Church in Exon.

> Chequy or and g[ules] a ch[i]ef vairry or and b[lue]. S[i]r John Chichester, knight. This coate is in St Peter's in Exon.[2]

The relevance of these entries to the two knightly effigies, as we shall see, is supported by the evidence of later witnesses.

Three other writers described the knights in the first half of the seventeenth century. They were Sir William Pole, who researched and wrote a description of Devon before his death in 1635, and two visitors to Exeter: Lieutenant Hammond from Norwich in 1635 and Richard Symonds in 1644. Pole, the earliest of the three, records that

> Twoe knightes lye together in the wall which devideth the quire and the ambulatory, the on with the armes of Bohun on his shield, and the other with the armes of Ralegh, of Ralygh: vid[elicet] Checque, Or and Geules, a chief verry.[3]

Hammond states,

> Beyond the Quire on that side next the wall, lyes 2. old warriors in Marble, the one is Bohun Earl of Hereford, in his Coat of Maile, with his sword, and Target, in his crosse legg'd Posture.

> The other is one Chichester, an old knight of the Rhodes in his Armour Cap a pee: and in the same cross-legg'd posture.[4]

Richard Symonds describes

> One lying crosst-legged, drawing a sword, and a shield on his left arme painted.

> Checky gules and or, a chief vair for Chichester, who had a brother, bishop of the church.

> Next to him another of the same forme, Bohun.

> A cap, like a helme, lying under his head; no creast.

Epitaphium D. Bohunni Illustrissimi Quondam Comitis Herefordensis.[5]

There is no need to list descriptions of the knights after this date, because later observers had no further evidence before them and may just have copied what earlier writers had noted.

Putting our five authorities together, we see that three of them believed the knight on the left to be Chichester and one to be Ralegh. Three agreed that his neighbour on the right was Bohun. In the case of Bohun there is significance in the Latin phrase with which Symonds concludes his account. This was not his invention but the title of an inscription placed, by the 1640s, on the wall behind the monument. The inscription was still readable at the end of the eighteenth century, when the historian Richard Polwhele transcribed it along with six lines of Latin verse that followed it – lines lamenting the fate of Earl Humphrey de Bohun, who was killed in Yorkshire in 1322 while rebelling against Edward II.[6] Polwhele thought that the inscription was composed by John Hooker (died 1601), the Exeter chamberlain and historian, and this may well be true. The verses are in the style of the Renaissance, not of the middle ages, and they cannot have been there in Leland's time or he would have mentioned them. They were probably added to the tomb in the late sixteenth or early seventeenth century, and they fit with Hooker's interest in the cathedral as well as in Exeter's links with famous people and national events.

It does not take long to realise that the monument cannot be Earl Humphrey's. He was buried in the Dominican Friary at York. Supporters of the Bohun theory have tried to get round this by arguing that the tomb is a 'cenotaph' or memorial.[7] They point out that Humphrey's daughter Margaret married Hugh Courtenay, earl of Devon, in 1325, and might have wished to have a monument to her father in the cathedral. Later, she and her husband were also buried there. But this suggestion lacks credibility too. When Margaret and Hugh got married, the Courtenay family did not have a close relationship with the cathedral. Their link was with Cowick

Priory outside Exeter where Hugh's grandfather was buried, and during the early years of their marriage his grandmother, mother, and father (who died between 1325 and 1340) were also buried there. The priory, not the cathedral, was the family mausoleum up to the middle of the fourteenth century.[8] As late as August 1376, when Earl Hugh made his will, he opted to be buried in Tiverton parish church, close to his principal residence. It was only in a codicil to his will, dated 28 April 1377, a few days before his death, that he changed his mind in favour of the cathedral, as a result of which he was buried there and joined by Margaret when she died in 1391.[9] There is no reason to suppose that she would have wished to set up a monument to her father in the cathedral during the 1320s, since it was not then a church with which she had a major connection.

We can get closer towards a solution by asking why the early antiquaries thought that the knight was a Bohun. There was no inscription to that effect, since Leland says nothing about the knight's identity, so the antiquaries can only have based their opinion on the knight's coat of arms – a coat that Pole claims to have been still visible. The best explanation is that they mistook a similar coat of arms for that of the Bohuns. After all, the monument was over 250 years old, and the shield might not have been renewed since it was first painted. And it so happens that somebody else both possessed a similar coat of arms and was connected with the cathedral at the right date. In the cathedral 'obit accounts' for Christmas term 1316–17, we read the following entry, in translation:

> Funeral money for the corpse of H. de Boxe, 8s. 0¾d., divided among the [fourteen] canons named below, each of whom received 7d. [by] adding 1¼d.

This is followed, after a short interval, by a second entry:

> For the palfrey of Henry de la Boxe, 40s., divided among the canons named below, each of whom [received] 2s. 10¼d., and there remains 0½d.[10]

The entries show that Henry de [la] Boxe had a funeral in the cathedral between Christmas 1326 and Easter 1327, at which the offerings came to just over 8s. together with the value of his horse.

We are not told this man's identity, but we are given clues to his rank. Funeral offerings worth 8s. indicate a relatively wealthy person with the status of a leading citizen or lesser member of the aristocracy. The offering of a horse was very unusual. The only other examples in the obit accounts relate to canons and to a knight, and as Boxe was certainly not a canon, he looks like a knight or at least a lesser member of the knightly class: what a century later would be called a 'gentleman'. The obit accounts relate to a funeral not a burial, so we cannot argue from them that Boxe was buried in the cathedral; he could have been taken for burial to one of the friaries. But as he was not seemingly a local resident who might have made connections with another church, and yet appears to have had links with the cathedral, a burial in the latter looks very likely.

The appearance of Henry de Boxe in the obit accounts would not bring to mind the 'Bohun' knight were it not for a piece of heraldic evidence. One of the most important records of heraldry in the early fourteenth century is the 'Great, Parliamentary, or Bannerets' Roll', drawn up in French between 1312 and 1314. It lists the coats of arms of the English aristocracy, from the king down to ordinary knights, the latter arranged by county. Under Surrey and Sussex, we read, in translation:

Sir Henri de Box, or six lioncels gules and a bend argent.[11]

Now this coat was remarkably like the Bohuns'. It had a bend of *argent* (silver) as its central feature – the same device and colour that they had, although in their case the bend was bordered by two thin lines or 'cotises' of *or* (gold). It featured six lioncels (small lions), probably three on either side of the bend like those of the Bohuns. There were differences of colour, the field (background colour) of the Box shield being *or* while that of the Bohuns was *azure* (blue), and the Box lioncels being *gules* (red) while those of the Bohuns were *or*. But the post-Reformation antiquaries were not necessarily as learned as we are. They would have known the Bohun coat well, while that of Box would have been much less familiar. They may have been confused by the colours, knowing that red was sometimes painted beneath gold leaf, or have assumed that the colours had been wrongly repainted. It would have been easy to suppose that what belonged to Box should be attributed to Bohun.

Was the Henry de Box of the shield the same as the Henry de Boxe of the funeral? The surname Box is not common in knightly circles, and there are other references to a person or persons of this name in the early fourteenth century who could well be both the knight and the corpse. Evidence of a Boxe family in Surrey and Sussex is elusive in this period; perhaps Henry was temporarily resident there in the service of a lord. Further west, however, Henry de Boxe held a quarter of a knight's fee in West Chickerell, Dorset, in 1285 and 1303; Henry de Boxe held Box, Wiltshire, in 1316; and Henry atte Boxe held a quarter of a fee in Skilgate, Somerset, in 1303, by gift of Robert FitzPayn – perhaps as a trustee for FitzPayn's family.[12] The last-named Henry presented a rector to the church of Skilgate in 1316, and was then described as Sir Henry de Boxe.[13] Finally, Henry, son of Sir Henry de Boxe, occurs owning land at Box, probably in Wiltshire, between 1336 and 1340.[14]

It is not clear if all these people were the same, but it seems likely that Sir Henry de Boxe the knight owned property at Box, Wiltshire, and had interests in Skilgate – the latter of which might have brought him close to Exeter. A further suggestive link with the cathedral comes from the fact that two men with the same surname were employed there at the time that Henry died. Robert Ataboxe (alias Boxe) was paid as a senior craftsman from 1317 to 1319 and Thomas Atteboxe from 1317 to 1318, but both may have been working before these dates since earlier accounts are lost.[15] Normally one would not think of a knight and craftsmen as being related, but the lack of much evidence about Henry's lands suggests that he belonged to a relatively humble gentry family. Alternatively Robert and Thomas may have come from Box without having been Henry's relations.

The time of his death, the winter of 1316–17, coincided with the great famine of 1315–17. There was a higher than usual mortality, caused partly by the famine and partly by the spread of disease as a consequence.[16] This could well have caused his death in the city. His family and friends were then in a good position to secure a tomb for him in the cathedral, and the Atteboxe craftsmen may even have made it. The fact that his family and coat of arms were not local to Exeter, however, would account for the lack of references to him or knowledge about him in later times. So while we cannot ascribe the tomb to him with absolute certainty, the evidence in his favour is far stronger and more likely than that of Humphrey de Bohun. He had a funeral in the right place at the right time, a coat of arms like that seen later on, and men with his surname were based at the cathedral.

The knight on the left-hand side raises a different set of problems. The coat of arms on the knight's shield, 'chequy or and gules, a chief vair', certainly belonged to the Chichester family of Raleigh, Devon, in the sixteenth century. But, as has often been pointed out, the arms were originally those of the Ralegh family of Raleigh, and passed with Raleigh and its property to the Chichesters through the marriage of the Ralegh heiress, Thomasine, to Sir John Chichester in about 1385.[17] His family had not hitherto had a significant presence in Devon. Sir William Pole, the best informed of our witnesses, was aware of this fact, and there can be little doubt that the heraldry of the tomb linked it with a Ralegh of Raleigh. Unfortunately for us the Ralegh family had several branches, whose genealogy has not been fully reconstructed and may be irrecoverable for the period when the tomb was made: the early fourteenth century.[18] The Ralegh who has been identified by modern historians as the owner of the tomb is Sir Henry who died in 1301. But this identification rests solely on their assumption that he was the only Ralegh with a link to the cathedral.

The unknown knight in the south choir aisle, most likely to be Sir Henry de Boxe

Sir Henry was the knight whose death in the Dominican Friary, Exeter, caused a serious dispute between the friars and the dean and chapter of the cathedral. Custom in Exeter dictated that all lay people should be taken to the cathedral for funeral rites, and buried in the cathedral cemetery unless permission for burial elsewhere was obtained from the chapter. Ralegh died while living with the Dominicans, and the friars prepared to give him funeral and burial in their church without the chapter's consent. Two of the cathedral canons, including Walter Stapledon (later bishop of Exeter) went to the friary with supporters and took away the body, despite the friars' protests. They carried it to the cathedral for funeral rites, and then returned it to the friary where the friars refused to accept it, so that the corpse lay outside in the street for some time. It was then buried in the cathedral. In 1306 the dean and chapter agreed to allow Sir Henry's body to be moved to another place if his widow and friends so desired, but the documentary evidence about the controversy does not state whether or not that happened.[19]

The historians A. G. Little and R. C. Easterling, who examined this episode carefully, concluded that 'it is probable that exhumation never took place, and that the body of Sir Henry de Ralegh still rests under his effigy in the cathedral'.[20] This conclusion, however, also presumes that the 'Ralegh' tomb belonged to Sir Henry. In truth we do not know, because the cathedral obit accounts make it possible that another Ralegh knight was buried in the building soon afterwards. The accounts begin to survive at Midsummer 1305 (too late to mention Sir Henry), but in Christmas term 1308–9 they refer to the funeral of Sir Thomas de Ralegh and state that his palfrey and arms were given to the cathedral as an offering.[21] Again the reference is to a funeral, not a burial. Sir Thomas could have been buried in some other local church, by arrangement with the dean and chapter, but we have to leave open the possibility that he was not and that the Ralegh tomb is in fact his, not Sir Henry's. Of the two, Sir Thomas was the more prominent. He was a justice of the peace, a commissioner in charge of royal forests, a collector of parliamentary taxation in Devon, and sheriff of the county in 1300 and 1307.[22]

Sir Henry's career is difficult to trace and to disentangle from that of a relative with a similar name.[23]

But that is not the end of the problem. The 'Ralegh' tomb was evidently put in its place after 'Boxe's', because its arch has slightly injured the arch of the latter. Since 'Boxe' is likely to date from 1317 or later, the 'Ralegh' monument must be later still. It can only relate to Sir Henry or Sir Thomas Ralegh if it was in some other place before 1317. That is a possibility, because this section of the choir wall would have been disturbed in 1327 when Bishop Berkeley's tomb was inserted, a little further east. Perhaps the Ralegh monument was moved further west at that time. If it has always been in its present position, then it must relate to yet another Ralegh, not recorded in cathedral records, or to another knight whose coat of arms was misread as that of Chichester in the sixteenth century. The question of the 'Ralegh' monument turns out to be like one of those tightly knotted skeins of parcel string that are impossible to find the ends of and to untie.

The third body is altogether different in form, but its identification involves the same kinds of difficulties. It is indeed the kind of corpse that figures in 'The Three Living and the Three Dead', and lies in the north wall of the north choir aisle, near the entrance to the chapels of St Andrew and St Katherine. The recess where it is placed has a richly carved vault, but there is nothing splendid about the effigy within it, which represents a naked man laid on a shroud, which his left hand has pulled across to hide his middle parts. His skin hangs loose on the shrunken flesh of his body, showing the bones beneath. A monument like this is known as a cadaver or transi and was popular in the fifteenth century, usually on tombs of clergy. At Canterbury and Wells there are examples of two-storey tombs, displaying a bishop in robes on an upper level and his corpse below.

The Exeter cadaver has only two identifying features today. These are shields carved with the arms of the cathedral and diocese, placed in the spandrels or corners of the recess arch. At the back of the recess are two uncarved shields, now plain but which Richard Symonds, on his visit in 1644, noted as displaying the arms of Edmund Lacy, bishop of Exeter from 1419 to 1455 (the heads of three shovellers or ducks).[24] Along the front of the recess are two lines of rhyming hexameters in Latin, a rough translation of which, preserving the rhyme-scheme, might be

> From this cold corpse be instructed, and from complacency wake you:
> You will by Death be abducted when he approaches to take you.

There is another cadaver tomb in the cathedral, that of Canon William Sylke in the north transept, and it carries a similar kind of warning. 'I am what you will be, and I was what you are.'

Two suggestions have been made about the figure's identity. In 1635 Hammond ascribed it to 'one Parkehouse, a canon'.[25] Nine years later Symonds thought it belonged to a 'brother of Bishop Lacy'.[26] Hammond's theory can be dismissed at once, because Canon William Parkehouse died in 1541, too late for the tomb, and was buried under a slab in the chapel of St Andrew. Symonds's conjecture is more promising, because Bishop Lacy had a married brother Philip, who served as a squire in his household. Philip died in the winter of 1444–5, the right period, and we know that he was buried in the cathedral.[27] However, Philip was too low in rank to have qualified for a monumental effigy – something allowed only to bishops and knights, not even to deans and canons. One would require more evidence before assigning the tomb to him.

A third possibility arises from the will of Canon William Browning, made in August 1454, a few months before his death in the following winter. In it he asked to be buried 'in the cathedral church at Exeter near the image which I have ordained at my own costs, in the ambulatory on the ground next to the entry to the exchequer of the aforesaid church'.[28] This careful instruction means, in modern terms, 'in the north

'Whose body?' The decaying corpse in the north choir aisle

choir aisle near the entrance to the chapels of St Andrew and St Katherine', just east of the cadaver tomb, and Browning's tomb slab now lies in the floor beside the cadaver itself. He owed his canonry to Bishop Lacy and Lacy was still alive when he died, so the presence of Lacy's coat of arms and those of the cathedral and the diocese would be appropriate on a monument set up by Browning.

There are problems, however, about the cadaver being his. He too was ineligible as a mere canon to have an effigy: the sole canon who managed to gain one was William Sylke, and he probably did so only by paying to install a new screen around the altar of the Holy Cross in the north transept, in return for which he was allowed to put his effigy into the screen. Browning might perhaps have got permission to erect a monument on the grounds that it was a teaching aid, telling people to prepare for death, rather than his own tomb; he, of course, was actually buried nearby beneath the pavement, not in the tomb. But the monument is remarkably elaborate for a teaching aid: a painting or wooden statue would have done as well.

A further theory is worth considering. This is that Lacy built the monument to be his own tomb. There is no evidence for this, but it would harmonise with the coats of arms. In about the 1430s or 40s Lacy would have realised that he would not be moved from Exeter to another see (his health was declining) and that he would be buried in the cathedral. Like previous bishops he would have planned his tomb. Originally bishops were buried in the choir, but this was full by 1326 and Lacy's three predecessors all had to be laid to rest in other parts of the building. The Lady Chapel too was more or less full by this time. A tomb in the north choir aisle, near the choir, may well have been Lacy's idea, and a cadaver monument would have been a likely choice for a man as pious as he. When Lacy died in 1455, however, he was reputed to be a saint. Almost certainly an earlier bishop (possibly Richard Blundy, whose resting place is unknown) was turned out of the choir to make room for Lacy, and he was buried on the north side of the choir beside the choir aisle in a plain altar tomb matching that of Bishop Berkeley on the opposite side of the choir, another bishop who – as we shall shortly see – had a saintly reputation. This would explain why Lacy was not, in the end, interred in the wall beneath the cadaver.

Of the candidates for the cadaver, therefore, we can dismiss Parkehouse and probably Philip Lacy. There is something to be said in favour of both Browning and Lacy, and also something against them. Browning set up an image in the right place, but it could have been some other kind of image, and he was buried near the cadaver not underneath it. Lacy could have planned his tomb as a cadaver and the coats of arms fit him, but his eventual tomb lay in another place. In one sense the identity of the body or its maker does not matter. What it shows us is that the clergy of Exeter Cathedral shared in the liking, common in England during the fifteenth century, for displaying images of death. This arose partly from a wish to appear humble and partly to warn people that they must prepare for a fate that none would escape. It is tempting to imagine this liking as typically medieval, but in fact it endured on tombs, in motifs such as skulls and skeletons, through Tudor and Stuart times and even into the eighteenth century.

5   ST JAMES OF EXETER

> Many kings have been made to sit on the ground;
> and one that was never considered has worn the crown.
> *Ecclesiasticus, Chapter 11*

The tomb of Bishop Lacy between the choir and the north choir aisle in Exeter Cathedral is a plain piece of work, topped by a much-scarred marble slab which once contained a brass but is now quite bare of ornament and identification. Lacy, who died in 1455, had a reputation for holiness, as we have seen. Pilgrims came to his tomb and prayed for his help in curing their ailments. But he was not the only bishop of Exeter to be honoured as a saint. Exactly opposite his resting place, on the south side of the presbytery, is another plain tomb with a similar marble top and missing brass. The modern visitor, and even the modern historian, hardly gives it a glance, but pilgrims in the early fourteenth century crowded around it as eagerly as their descendants did around Lacy's. It is the tomb of the sixteenth bishop of Exeter, James Berkeley, who died in 1327.

To understand how Berkeley, who was bishop for scarcely three months, became the object of a saint cult, we have to start with the history of England. In the autumn of 1326 Queen Isabella and her lover Roger Mortimer seized power from the unpopular King Edward II and his government. On 15 October Walter Stapledon, bishop of Exeter, treasurer of England and one of Edward's staunchest supporters, was intercepted by a mob in London and stabbed to death.[1] On 5 December the cathedral chapter of Exeter met to elect a new bishop, and they chose James Berkeley. It was a wise choice at a difficult time. By fourteenth-century standards, Berkeley had excellent qualifications. He was a nobleman of the Berkeley family in Gloucestershire, a doctor of theology, and a canon of the cathedral, although in recent years he had spent most of his time at Hereford Cathedral (of which he was also a canon) rather than at Exeter.[2]

Politically, James had the advantage of links with both the king's side and the queen's. He had been on good terms with Edward II, to whom he was distantly related, but his brother and nephew were in Isabella's party, which is how Edward, after being deposed in January 1327, came to be imprisoned in Berkeley Castle and murdered there in September. James's election was acceptable to the queen and the new government, and Berkeley was consecrated bishop at Canterbury on 22 March 1327. At about the same time, the body of Stapledon was brought from London and reburied in the magnificent tomb which its owner, when living, had prepared for himself beside the high altar. As for Berkeley, he ruled the diocese for only thirteen weeks. He died on 24 June at Peterhayes in Yarcombe parish, east Devon, one of the bishop of Exeter's manor houses, and was buried in the cathedral on the 27th. Three months later pilgrims were already flocking to his tomb, and Exeter had gained a saint – albeit an unofficial one.

Of the two bishops who were laid to rest in the cathedral in 1327, Stapledon was the obvious candidate to be acclaimed as a saint. He was the first English bishop to be murdered since Thomas Becket in 1170, and he had been a generous benefactor of the Church. He had founded Exeter College, Oxford, and had given large sums of money to help rebuild the cathedral. His family and friends grieved for his death. Prayers were organised, chantries were founded to pray for his soul, and even a monastery was planned in his memory. The general public in Devon was less favourable. 'A prophet is honoured, but not in his own country.' Stapledon was a local man of lowly stock, and he (and his family) had risen rapidly and to a high degree, sometimes at the expense of other people. People in Exeter may have remembered his high-handedness in snatching the body of Sir Henry de Ralegh from the Dominican Friary in 1301, discussed in the previous chapter. The Cornish, we are told, plundered Stapledon's property in Cornwall after his murder in London. Most people may have thought of him as the crony of the discredited Edward II, rather than a good bishop who came to a tragic end. Like heroes on quests in fairy stories, the public passed by Stapledon's rich and splendid monument in favour of the plain tomb modestly prepared for his successor. It was there that prayers were offered, candles lit, and miracles experienced. 'God moves in a mysterious way his wonders to perform.'

It is harder to explain why Berkeley was seen as a saint than why Stapledon was not. Well born, well educated, and well provided with Church benefices, there were many like him in the fourteenth century: grand figures of this world rather than the next. No doubt there was more to Berkeley than that. Our knowledge of most medieval bishops is limited to a list of their appointments and activities, which tells us little or nothing about their characters or personalities. Berkeley must have been pious, kindly, charitable, or ascetic to have stirred the veneration that followed his death. Snatched from this world a few weeks after coming to Exeter, he was able, like Pope John Paul I, to make a good first impression while escaping the disenchantment and unpopularity which usually follow. Political events in England were probably also helpful to his cult. The country was in a state of alarm and disturbance. The king had been deposed and murdered – something unheard of and horrifying. The new king, Edward III, was only fourteen, and as the Bible said (and people so often repeated), 'woe to the land where the king is a child'.[3] Isabella and Mortimer were not reassuring figures, and there were strained relations between them and the rest of the aristocracy, leading to unrest and disorder. In times of trouble people often look to saints for help and protection, and many saint-cults have started in such times.

The earliest evidence for Berkeley's cult comes on 30 September 1327 when the clerk of the cathedral exchequer noted the receipt of £3 13s. 'for wax at the tomb of Bishop James' – in other words for the offering of votive candles during the last three months.[4] The pilgrims evidently began to gather soon after the bishop's death, and further receipts of wax-money show that a few continued to come in the autumn and winter, although this time of the year was not popular for pilgrimages because of the poor state of the roads. But with the arrival of spring in 1328, there was a rush of people from the surrounding area to visit Berkeley's tomb. Whitsunday and the following three days were a traditional time for lay folk to offer money in the cathedral. In 1328 when Whitsuntide fell on 22 May, £5 was given in Whitsuntide offerings, but nearly £8 in offerings to Bishop Berkeley. Sales of wax for the year reached nearly £13, other monetary offerings may well have totalled £7–£14, and altogether it seems likely that £28–£35 (a large sum) was deposited for Berkeley in this, the peak year of enthusiasm.

The accounts do not tell us who the visitors were, or where they came from. But they evidently streamed along the Sidmouth road, past the little chapel of Clyst Gabriel at Bishop's Clyst, for its collecting box received more donations than usual, and at least one group of pilgrims came from outside Devon. News of the cult reached Berkeley Castle, and the bishop's nephew, Thomas Lord Berkeley, rode with his household to attend the cathedral on the anniversary of James's death. He offered money at the tomb, and his clerk, writing down the record of expenses, noted that it was given for 'Saint James de Berkeley'—as the bishop now looked like becoming.[5]

'Looked like', but did not. Although ordinary people believed in Berkeley's holiness, the cathedral authorities seem to have been more sceptical. 'How', we can imagine them saying, 'can Berkeley be a saint – a man so like ourselves?' Their attitude to his holiness is eloquently expressed by their silence about it. The cathedral kept a chronicle, mainly confined to recording bishops' deaths; it mentions Berkeley's, but says nothing about his life or his cult. One of the canons, Adam Murimuth, was writing a larger history of public events; he too included Berkeley's death without any comment. Berkeley's successor as bishop was John Grandisson, but he also virtually ignored the cult in his letters and writings. Once, perhaps, he made a complimentary remark in a letter to the earl of Devon who had complained that Berkeley owed him money. 'If he does not pay you in this world, you must hope as we do to find treasure through his prayers in heaven.' But he forbade the cathedral clergy to offer incense at any bishop's tomb unless the person was canonised, and he got angry in 1341 when the cathedral bells were rung to celebrate a miracle.[6]

Both reactions must have been caused by Berkeley's devotees. With regard to the miracle, the bishop was right for once, because the man involved (named John the Skinner) later admitted that his 'cure' from blindness was a bogus one, but it looks as though Grandisson regarded the whole Berkeley cult as hysterical and misconceived. The cathedral staff did not turn away the pilgrims or refuse their offerings, which produced useful sums for rebuilding the nave. But not until 1342, fifteen years after Berkeley's death, did the clergy belatedly

Bishop Berkeley's tomb in the south choir aisle

transfer a few shillings from the offerings to finance an annual mass in memory of James himself.

It is not unusual for new saints to encounter scepticism and hostility. To break this barrier two things are necessary: popular enthusiasm and official support. Berkeley had the first but not the second, just as Stapledon had the second but not the first. People continued to gather at Berkeley's tomb after 1328, to offer money and light candles, but no one took up the cause of applying for his canonisation, and the Church authorities maintained their aloofness. Very gradually, the popular cult declined. It lasted during the 1330s and 40s, but with the Black Death of 1349 many of the original devotees died, and the next generations developed different interests. A few people went on frequenting the tomb, but by the 1370s and 80s the cult was virtually extinct. Eventually there were not enough offerings even to pay for the bishop's memorial mass and that too was discontinued.

What did the cult achieve? There was the spiritual enthusiasm, which though short-lived was real. More solidly, at least £200 was transferred from the pilgrims' gifts to help rebuild the cathedral. The present nave could not have been finished so quickly, or to such a high standard, without the Berkeley cult. Some memory must also have survived. When Lacy, the next holy bishop, died, it can hardly be an accident that he was buried opposite Berkeley in an identical tomb. As a result, by a very appropriate piece of symmetry, the two bishops lie on either side of the presbytery: both Gloucestershire men and both (of all the Exeter bishops) the ones who came nearest to sainthood, in the popular view at least.

6 THE LADY OF THE SWANS

Here lies a most beautiful lady,
Light of step and heart was she;
I think she was the most beautiful lady
That ever was in the West Country.
Walter De La Mare, 'Epitaph'

The tomb of the earl and countess of Devon, in the south transept of the cathedral, is one of the best in the cathedral but one of the least well sited. It was not meant to stand here (which is no doubt why it looks forlorn and out of place), but between two pillars in the nave, opposite the pulpit. Originally, it lay inside a small chantry chapel and the figures on the tomb looked towards the altar of this chapel, as those of Bishops Stafford and Oldham still do in theirs. The chapel, however, was taken down after the Reformation, and the monument was moved to its present position in 1864 to make room for nave seating. On the tomb lie two idealised figures: the earl, a robust knight in armour, bearded in the fashion of the court of Edward III, and the countess, a young bride in a cloaked and sleeveless gown. In fact he was nearly seventy-four at his death in 1373, and she was probably at least in her late seventies when she followed him from this world in 1391.

The pillows of the earl and countess are supported by angels – symbols of salvation – and the earl's feet rest on a large and sturdy lion. But if you look beyond the lady's feet you will see something sad: a pair of swans, their necks entwined for comfort or protection and drooping for sorrow. Their beaks hold down a scroll whose words no longer survive. Around the neck of each swan is a metal collar to which a chain is attached, and these chains are not simply heraldic embellishments; they are part of the story I shall tell. There are many crests and badges in the cathedral in the forms of birds and animals, but the swans are rather unusual. They were an emblem of the countess's own family, the Bohuns, and the emblem was chosen to make a statement about the history of the family and its romantic origins. For the reason why the Bohuns displayed this badge was that *they claimed to be descended from a family of swans*!

Few women were buried in Exeter Cathedral during the middle ages. We know of at least one other lady of rank, Elizabeth Speke, who lies with her husband in the Speke chapel. Bishop Stapledon brought in his mother and father, and there were two or three wives of citizens of Exeter. The countess of Devon, however, was by far the most distinguished of these women, being the granddaughter of a king and the daughter, wife, and mother of earls. No other woman before the Reformation, as far as we know, was allowed the honour of an effigy of herself in the cathedral. She was Margaret, daughter of Humphrey de Bohun, earl of Hereford and Essex, and his wife Elizabeth whose father was Edward I. The date of her birth does not appear to be known, but since she married Hugh Courtenay, later earl of Devon, in 1325, she was probably born not later than 1313 because a permanent marriage could not be made until one reached the age of puberty – twelve in the case of girls. She may have been a year or two older, but not much older, because high aristocratic women often married in their early or mid-teens. Sometimes they began to bear children too early, and Lady Margaret Beaufort never recovered her fertility after giving birth to Henry VII at the age of fourteen. But Margaret's constitution was a strong one. She bore her husband seventeen children – eight boys and nine girls – and survived to a good age even by modern standards.[1]

So how did Margaret come to be linked with swans? The answer relates to a story written down in northern France in the thirteenth century called *The Birth of the Knight of the Swan*, which forms part of a larger cycle of tales about the great crusading hero Godfrey de Bouillon, who died in 1100.[2] The purpose of the swan story was to explain Godfrey's ancestry, and it began with two people who were alleged to have been his great-grandparents: King Oryens and his queen Beatrice. The story tells how Beatrice gave birth to septuplets, six boys and a girl, each born with a silver chain around the neck. The king's wicked mother, Matebrune, who hated the queen, ordered a servant to destroy the babies and to replace them with puppies.

On learning that his wife had given birth to animals, the king was horrified and put her into prison. A hermit rescued the babies and brought them up, but Matebrune heard of their survival and sent a forester named Mauquarre to take away their chains and kill them. When he took off their chains they turned into swans, except for the eldest boy who was not present. Mauquarre went back with the chains, and Matebrune ordered them to be made into a cup. The goldsmith she employed found that half of one chain sufficed for this, and hid the rest; the other half chain was given to Mauquarre.

Twelve years passed, and the wicked mother-in-law persuaded the king to burn his imprisoned wife. An angel carried news of this to the surviving twelve-year-old son, and told him to go and fight in his mother's defence. The boy had been brought up in seclusion; he had not been baptised or ever encountered a horse, but he went to the court where he was christened Elias in the French version, Eneas in English ones. The king gave him a steed and armour, including a shield marked with a cross, and in due course he was put to challenge Mauquarre. When the latter struck the cross on the shield, an adder sprang from it and attacked him, and flame gushed out and blinded him. Eneas then killed him. Beatrice was rescued, Matebrune burnt, and the goldsmith restored the chains that he had taken. After these were put back on the

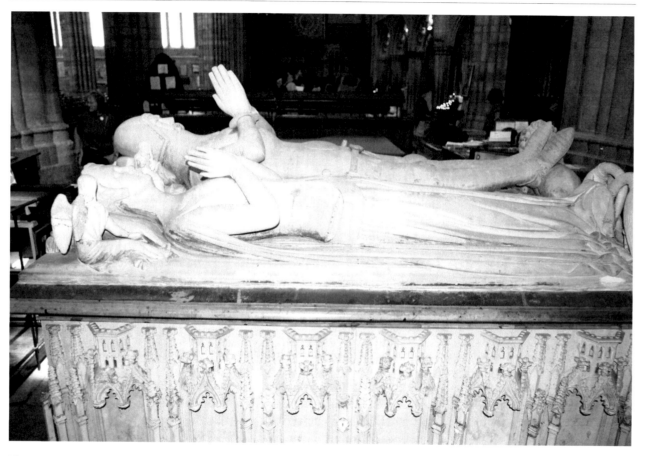

The earl and countess of Devon on their tomb in the south transept

The mourning swans at the feet of the countess

swans, they changed into children again, but because the chain of the last boy-swan was missing, that boy was condemned to remain a swan for ever.

Eneas then had further adventures, and eventually got married to a second Beatrice, the daughter of the Emperor Otto of Germany. He told his wife, however, that she must never ask about his origin or family. They had one child, a daughter Ide or Idein, who eventually married Eustace, count of Boulogne, and became the mother of three famous knights: Godfrey de Bouillon, Baldwin (later king of Jerusalem), and Eustace. But when at last Beatrice could not resist asking Eneas about his origins, he left her and eventually departed from the world in a boat drawn by his swan-brother – a story adapted by Wagner, with different names, for his opera *Lohengrin*. The cycle of crusading stories became extremely popular, especially in France but also in England; indeed it was known even in Exeter by the middle of the thirteenth century. This is shown by the fact that one of the misericords in the choir shows a helmeted knight in a boat being pulled by a swan.

The story was not just a story, however. It was adopted as an historical fact by a number of noble families in Flanders, Germany, and England who claimed to be descended from the swan knight and his wife.[3] The earliest such family in England was probably that of Tony, lords of Flamstead, Hertfordshire, which was descended from Eustace, count of Boulogne, who died in 1044. The last male Tony died in 1309 and his sister then married Guy de Beauchamp, with the result that their claim passed to Guy's family, the earls of Warwick. The Bohuns acquired a similar claim as a result of the marriage of Margaret's grandfather, Humphrey de Bohun, in 1275 to Maud, daughter of the count of Fiennes, near Calais, and the son of this marriage – Margaret's father – evidently took it seriously because he gave the name Eneas to one of her brothers, a boy who did not grow up to adulthood.[4] Through Margaret's marriage, the claim also passed to the members of the Courtenay family and (through marriage) to the Luttrells and the Carys, and it was still alive at the end of the sixteenth century.

As a result, the swan story continued to be well-known in England. There is a fifteenth-century version of it in Middle English, complete in itself, called *Chevalere Assigne*, 'the knight of the swan'.[5] When the historian of the earls of Warwick, John Rous, drew his well-known pictorial roll of the earls and their history in 1483–4, he included Eneas as one of their ancestors, placing him roughly in the Anglo-Saxon period. He also told the story on the roll with one or two differences, describing the chains as gold and Eneas as seven, not twelve. Rous added that Matebrune's cup was still preserved at Warwick Castle, and said that the countess of Warwick had allowed him to drink from it.[6]

In 1512, Robert Copland made a fresh translation of the original story into English prose, which was printed at least three times during the course of the sixteenth century. He did this at the order of Edward Stafford, duke of Buckingham, who was the most important descendant of the Bohuns at that time and who probably saw the story as a way of promoting his own family. The Copland version varies in some respects, notably in smoothing one of the most heart-rending parts of the earlier tale: the failure of the sixth boy to escape from the form of a swan. In the revised account, two cups have been made from the swans' chains. The children's mother dreams that if she can get two priests to celebrate mass using the cups as chalices, and places the swan on a bed between them, he will be restored to human form. This is done and that part of the story ends happily, the boy becoming a knight himself with the name of Emery.[7]

The fate of the chief swan families in England was less fortunate. The male line of the Bohuns ended in 1373, leaving two daughters, one of whom married Henry IV and the other his uncle Thomas. Thomas was murdered by Richard II, and three of his descendants, dukes of Buckingham, also died violent deaths, the last of them (Edward Stafford) at the hands of Henry VIII. Four of Henry IV's descendants came to similar ends, and the last earl of Warwick was the unfortunate boy kept in the Tower by Henry VII and executed by him in 1499. The sculptor of Margaret's tomb knew nothing of all this, and he probably made his swans look sad to act as mourners of her death, but the subsequent ill-fortune of so many of the English swan children shows that the real lives of the great and famous can be as tragic as any legend.

7 BOYS WILL BE BOYS

Choristers, do not spare,
Children too everywhere,
But like angels declare
'Praise to You, descending
For our souls' befriending!'
Carol: Personent Hodie

Think of cathedrals and you will probably think of choristers. Indeed hardly anything else about cathedrals, apart from their buildings, makes such an impression on people outside. We like children and (to an extent) cathedral music and we build a romance from the two, especially at Christmas time. Still, choristers deserve their popularity. They, or boys of a similar kind, go back as far as our cathedrals do. When Exeter Cathedral was founded in 1050, the rule that Bishop Leofric gave the clergy to guide them took it for granted that they would employ some boys, and laid down rules about their supervision.[1]

By the thirteenth century there were fourteen choristers at Exeter, living in ways that differed in several respects from that of their modern successors. They boarded at the cathedral, living in a building opposite the west front of the cathedral, long-since demolished. There they slept together in a dormitory and were taught to read and sing in a schoolroom by the succentor – the cleric in charge of the day-to-day work of the choir. For feeding purposes they were each attached to one of the resident canons. They went to their canon's house for meals, and counted as a kind of junior servant in his household. In the cathedral services they were treated as apprentice clergy. They sang plainsong in the choir along with the adults, but for a long time they did not contribute much that was special to the services except to do small tasks such as carrying holy water or books in processions.

Until about the middle of the fifteenth century choristers were probably chosen as much for their family links with the cathedral as for having particularly good voices. But at about that time, as polyphonic or harmonised music became popular in churches, it was realised that boys could make a unique contribution to such music by extending the range of the voices. Accordingly they began to be selected for their vocal quality and to receive special musical training from the clerk of the Lady Chapel, where most of the polyphony took place. When the Lady Chapel services were abolished in 1548, the post of clerk turned into that of master of the choristers, setting up the system to which we are used today.[2]

Medieval people shared our sentimental regard for choristers, especially during the Christmas season. A special role was given to the boys at matins on Christmas Day, or rather Christmas Night since matins was a night service. Towards the end of the first lesson at matins, a boy chosen for his good clear voice and dressed in a white alb with an amice or hood around his neck, appeared from behind the high altar and stood on the highest altar step, facing the altar and holding a lighted torch in his left hand. When the lesson was finished, he turned to face the choir and began to sing in Latin, 'On this day the King of Heaven, from a Virgin, consented to be born for us.' At 'King of Heaven' he raised his right hand to heaven, at 'from a Virgin' he extended it to the image of the Virgin Mary on the north side of the altar, and at 'consented to be born' he bowed his knee. The rest of the choir replied 'That he should call home outcast man to the kingdom of heaven'. Meanwhile three other choristers from the south side of the choir and three from the north, dressed in the same way, came to the lowest step of the altar. The first boy descended to join them, and all seven faced the choir, singing together *Gloria in excelsis deo*. 'Glory to God on high and in earth peace, goodwill towards men.'[3]

The high point of the choristers' year came three days after Christmas on 28 December, which we call Holy Innocents' Day and they knew as 'Childermas', 'the festival of the [Holy] Children'. This was the day of the 'boy-bishop', on which the choristers took over the chief role in the cathedral services from the adult clergy. The ceremonies began at vespers during the afternoon of the previous day, the 27th, when the boy-bishop, wearing a mitre and gloves and holding a pastoral staff, led the service and delivered a Latin blessing to the clergy in the choir and to the laity watching in the nave:

> I sign you with the sign of the cross. May your defence be He who bought
> you and redeemed you with the price of his flesh!

After this he returned to the choir and sat in a special place – presumably on the bishop's throne itself. For the next twenty-four hours he was nominally in charge of the services, although not necessarily present at them all, until vespers on the 28th when he gave a further blessing and laid down his office.[4]

Almost every church in medieval England had a boy-bishop until the custom was forbidden by Henry VIII in 1541.[5] Some functioned on St Nicholas Day, 6 December, some on the 28th, and some perhaps on both. There grew up on these days something of the atmosphere of an office-party, in which not only the boys but the adult clergy and the canons' servants let off steam with games and disorders in an escape from the routine of the rest of the year. Some of this happened in church and some outside. Boys in particular went round begging for money for their bishop, sometimes with such energy that the term 'St Nicholas's clerks' came to be a slang term for highway robbers. Shakespeare uses it of Falstaff and his gang in *Henry IV Part 1*.

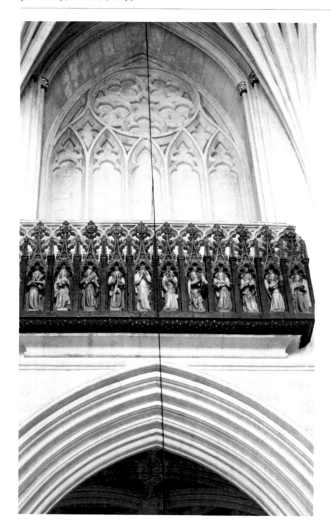

The most elaborate money raising was done at York Minster, where the boy-bishop and his fellow choristers spent a good deal of January on journeys on horseback through Yorkshire to places as far away as Northallerton and Doncaster. They visited the local gentry and the neighbouring abbeys, and collected as much as £8 15s. Much of this they used for feasting – on one occasion tucking in to chickens, ducks, woodcocks, fieldfares, and a plover, followed by honey, pears, and wine. The boy-bishop took the balance of just over £2 for himself: a useful sum for his schooling or career.

The festivities at Exeter also included meals, journeys, and begging, at least around the city, but on a smaller scale than at York. What we know about this comes from some regulations which were issued, probably by the dean and chapter of the cathedral between about 1450 and 1530, in an effort to curb the disorder and extravagance that the festival tended to cause.[6] When the boy-bishop was chosen, the canon to whom he belonged, his 'master', became responsible for some of the jollifications that

The 'minstrels' gallery'. Its use is obscure, but it is possible that choristers sometimes sang there

went on, and it seems that some canons begrudged the expenses to which they were put – hence the regulations.

Normally the choristers went to breakfast with their own canons, but on 28 December they had a communal breakfast in 'the chamber of the bishop': some special room, perhaps even a chamber in the real bishop's palace. The regulations cut down the breakfast to a few pennyworth of bread, meat, cheese, or butter, with small beer to drink, after which the boys set out on a journey to St Nicholas Priory, off Fore Street, where the monks probably gave them money or refreshments. The journey would have been made with some ceremony, the boy-bishop in his pontifical robes preceded by his cross-bearer, and other churches or houses may have been visited too. Meanwhile, junior clergy from the cathedral distributed gloves in the close and the boy-bishop's canon's servants did so in the city, apparently as gifts to canons and other important people and very likely in return for donations.

At about midday the boys came back and the boy-bishop's canon provided a special dinner in his house. This seems to have been lavish at times, in terms of the food provided and the number of guests entertained, and the regulations cut back the dinner severely. There were to be only six guests from among the 'friends' (meaning the family) of the boy-bishop, and the boy had to pay 4d. for each of their dinners if his canon so requested. One hopes, although we are not told, that all the choristers came to the dinner too. After dinner there would have been the service of vespers in church, at which the boy-bishop gave up his office.

On one or other evening, the 28th or 29th, the boys' celebrations seem to have involved the vicars choral who, by the fifteenth century, lived in their little street of buildings in Kalendarhay, the hall of which still stands as a ruin alongside South Street. But the regulations stopped this, warning that 'no carrying of wine or a torch to Kalendarhay shall be done'. They also forbade the boys to have a second special breakfast on the 29th, St Thomas's Day, or to spend the following days going around the city with presents of gloves, although it was conceded that this could be done if important people were in town for a county court meeting or the sessions of justices of the peace.

Arrangements were also made about the money collected in church and around the city These were to go to the boy-bishop, but he was banned from paying anything to the other choristers – no doubt to stop them pressing him for a share. To ensure this, the offerings were to be counted (by the boys?) in front of the cathedral staff and entrusted to a member of the boy-bishop's family to be kept for his benefit.

We know the names of some 87 choristers up to the middle of the sixteenth century, mostly from the 1310s and 20s and the 1530s and 40s, but this is a very small fraction of the number who existed.[7] In the latter period the money earned by each chorister was kept in a purse and given to him when he left the choir, in return for him or his father signing a 'release' in which they gave up any further claim on the cathedral. Some thirty-three of these 'choristers' releases' survive, and they are interesting in throwing light on the boys' social origins.[8] In fourteen cases where the parents are identified, two fathers were described as gentlemen (one having sired his son out of wedlock), one as a merchant, two as yeomen, and five as husbandmen meaning peasant farmers. The rest were a brewer, a miller, a weaver, and a widow. The boys came not only from Exeter but Alphington, Bradninch, Okehampton, and even Tavistock, so widely across the county.

What happened to them in the end? By the early sixteenth century, boys with good voices were highly sought after and liable to be 'poached' by other choirs. In 1531–2 the dean and chapter paid 10s. to Robert Phillips of Henry VIII's chapel royal, who came on a talent-spotting tour, and gave him a further 15s. in 1534–5.[9] These may have been 'sweeteners' to persuade him not to take away any boys. The cathedral valued the help that the choristers gave them, and was willing to keep them on the staff when their voices broke. When that happened they became eligible to be promoted as secondaries, to sit in the middle row of the choir, and to attend the city High School.

In later life some became clergy and got posts at the cathedral or in country parishes. Others preferred to leave and take up lay employment. One of the latter, Robert Chave, who came from Wellington, Somerset, rose to be mayor of Exeter. So the choristers, then as now, were free to choose their adult careers and made various choices, but the years they spent at the cathedral must often have left its mark upon them, just as is true today.

THE REGULATIONS FOR HOLY INNOCENTS' DAY [10]
(Translated from Latin)

No carrying of wine or a torch to Kalendarhay shall be done on the vigil of St Thomas the Apostle.

No breakfast shall be had on the day of St Thomas the Apostle in the chamber of the chorister bishop, but the bishop along with the choristers and the canons' servants shall go to the house of their masters, as they are accustomed to go on other days.

The distribution of gloves within the close shall be done by two or three [who wear] the habit of the choir, and in the city and the suburbs by two, three, or four of the servants of the canon [who is] master of the bishop, appointed after the discretion of the said master.

The bishop shall give no reward to his brother choristers on Holy Innocents' Day.

None shall be called to dinner on Holy Innocents' Day at the expense of the bishop to the house of his master unless they are special friends of the said bishop, and then not beyond the number of six persons. In this case the bishop shall pay his canon master, if the latter wishes to receive it, 4*d*. for the dinner of each person thus present. And the bishop shall deem himself content with the service of his master.

Provision shall be made on Holy Innocents' Day by the canon master of the bishop that the servants of his lord bishop may cause to be ordained and prepared one pennyworth of bread, one pottle [four pints] of small beer, and two or three pennyworth of meat or one pennyworth of cheese or butter. These they shall bring to the chamber of the bishop at the time of '*Preciosa*'[11] where the bishop and his brother choristers shall consume them together immediately, and [then] he shall go down to the priory of St Nicholas. The expense of the aforesaid breakfast shall not exceed the sum of four or six pence.

It is ordained that both the said bishop and his cross-bearer shall attend the choir and the school on the days after the aforesaid feast of Holy Innocents, along with the rest of the choristers, and that they do not run about through the church or other places with gloves, unless the county [court] or the sessions of the peace are held in Exeter, or when it happens that some honest and extraneous person happens to come to the church or to the house of some canon on other days during the aforesaid time of the year. And even this [shall be done] only with the licence of the precentor or the succentor or the clerk of the chapel of the Blessed Mary.

Also that the money offered to the bishop on Innocents' Day shall be openly counted without delay within the church in front of one of the clerks of the exchequer or of some honest priest [wearing] the habit of the choir, deputed by the canon master of the bishop, and then let the money be safeguarded by one of the friends of the bishop.

8 AN EXETER SCHOOLROOM IN THE FIFTEENTH CENTURY

I would my master were an hare
And that his books all hounds were,
And I myself a jolly hunter;
To blow my horn I would not spare,
For if he were dead I would not care!
Fifteenth-Century Schoolboy's Song

Choristers went to school, at least to be taught to sing. What else did the cathedral do to promote education? There was no cathedral school in the modern sense; no school for members of the public. Even the choristers, it seems, were taught on their own. Few English cathedrals had public schools closely attached to them until Henry VIII established his King's Schools in the 1540s at Canterbury, Ely, and elsewhere. The nearest thing to a cathedral school in medieval Exeter was the High School, a name that meant the chief school of the city. The High School had a relationship with the cathedral, but a semi-detached one. Its schoolmaster was appointed by the archdeacon of Exeter (who was a member of the cathedral chapter), and some of the masters were former members of the cathedral staff. The buildings, after 1344, were cared for by the cathedral, and the teenaged youths on its staff – the secondaries – were sent to the school to learn Latin.

However, the High School was not sited at the cathedral. In the thirteenth century, when we first hear about its location, it lay in Preston Street, 'the street of the priests', where one presumes that the parish clergy of the city once lived. Later, in 1344, the dean of the cathedral, Richard Braylegh, gave the school new buildings in an alley off the High Street known as Christchurch Lane, a few yards west of the entrance to Castle Street.[1] Not only was the school at some distance from the cathedral, but most of its pupils would have come not from there but from the city and the surrounding county. The school was for older boys and it charged fees, flourishing on this basis until 1631 when the city council founded Exeter School, also for boys, on the opposite side of the High Street. Exeter School offered free education and the High School became less popular. It lingered for a long time but ceased to operate in 1750. The dean and chapter at that time saw no need for it to continue and the cathedral has not had a close link with a place of secondary education since then. The present Cathedral School for younger children is largely a creation of the Victorians.

We know a good deal about medieval schools.[2] In the case of the High School this includes the sites, the names of many of the masters, some even of those of the pupils, and, perhaps most precious of all, notebooks kept by three of them during the fifteenth century. These books enable us to see what they studied and how they did so. The grammars and vocabularies used for learning Latin in those days are a difficult, technical subject to explain, but one of the notebooks – now in the library of Caius College, Cambridge – contains some more appealing material. This is a set of 82 short passages of Latin prose, dating from about the 1440s.[3] They are exercises in composing Latin, and many of them refer to the life of the school, the interests of the schoolboys, and events in the world outside. The schoolmaster at the time was John Borington, a former secondary of the cathedral, who was also vicar of the church of St Mary Major in the cathedral close. The pupil who copied the work was named William Berdon. It is difficult to be sure whether the exercises were devised by the schoolmaster or composed by the pupil, but that scarcely matters. Reading them gives a vivid sense of being in Exeter just before the start of the Wars of the Roses.

Most of the boys in the school were probably aged from about ten to eighteen. Very likely, they learnt to read in smaller private schools before going on to the High School to be taught Latin. Some Exeter girls may have been taught in private schools as well. The exercises give us a few glimpses about the kinds of pupils who went to the High School. One boy is said to have come from Totnes; another declares that his parents live in the country with a large family and are hard put to support him at school in Exeter. A third claims or imagines that he is a lord's son who wears silk, satin, damask, and velvet on festival days, while in a fourth case a boy is described as the son of a widow. Some older boys of modest means earned money by acting as the parish clerks of the Exeter parish churches, serving at mass and ringing bells, but it seems that the pay was poor. One passage observes ruefully that parish clerks lose rather than gain a living from their jobs. 'Today we have received an outstanding reward for bell-ringing: three halfpennies and a farthing's worth of thin ale.'

The school would have been housed in an oblong hall, not unlike the main room of a large house. The master would have had a large seat on the inner narrow wall and his assistant or 'usher' a smaller one by the door. The boys would have sat on benches round the room, facing inwards. The school day, like the working day at that time, began early, and a seven o'clock start is mentioned as being unduly late! Lessons probably commenced at six and went on for a couple of hours before breakfast, with a further break for late-morning dinner at eleven or twelve and departure in the late afternoon. But as the school had only two staff, strict timekeeping was not always observed. The master was often slow to arrive, prompting the scholars to do the same. Unfortunately, on the morning when they came at seven, he was already there to give them a beating, and on another occasion, when they reckoned that he would be late, he was unexpectedly early. They speculated that he had been woken by cats, or had not had a good drink before he went to bed. At times, the master was absent during the day; twice there are complaints that the boys had no work to do in consequence.

In other respects, the school was organised like a modern one. There were three or four terms in the year and examinations were held at the end of term. School work included the reading, writing, and speaking of Latin, and a word that constantly occurs in the exercises is *opposicio*. This had two meanings: examination, in which you were verbally quizzed by the master about your knowledge, and disputation, in which two or more scholars argued why points of grammar and style were correct – a good training for university or a career in law.

The master also tried to teach good manners. A number of the exercises attack vice and praise the importance of virtue. The scholars are urged to heed wise counsel, be humble and grateful to their parents, and pray devoutly. They should avoid boasters and flatterers, and try to tame the wildness of human nature. One passage summarises the laws of life as living honestly, not hurting others, and respecting their rights. Teachers in early schools made copious use of corporal punishment and Master Borington, although a clergyman, was apparently no different in this respect. Boys were beaten for arriving late and even for carelessly falling down in the lane outside. One boy, on a cold morning, says that he has had three hard beatings on his buttocks. It may have been the master who dictated the rest of the sentence: this will warm him up and be a good omen for the rest of the day!

Some pupils sought to escape from the class by playing truant. 'Every day when the scholars begin to be examined in Latin composition, one of the company goes out of the door with furtive steps, unknown to the master, because he will not wait to settle accounts with that formidable man.' In summer time, the lure of the fields was irresistible. 'If our group of six or seven are questioned, let's all reply by boasting that we had a good appetite to eat and drink and went into the woods, searching for leaves and flowers.' Those who remained in the classroom dreamed about food – dreams encouraged by the master, one feels, because he could use the subject to teach them obscure Latin words relating to the menu.

In the weeks after Christmas, the boys could imagine capons, pheasants, and partridges being fattened for eating before the start of Lent. When Lent was over, they could think of other dainty dishes. 'Today, I shall not eat meat or fish but I shall fare well, by God's grace, on stuffed tripes, puddings, chitterlings, sausages, and haggises which some people eat on Wednesdays.' The boy represented as coming from Totnes boasts of its fish, 'the best trout in the whole kingdom, so they say, and if only we might have three or four of them tomorrow for dinner!' Summer brought with it the promise of 'beans, peas, strawberries, cherries, and wild pears for sale in the market'.

An important season in the culinary cycle was Rogationtide: the Monday, Tuesday and Wednesday before Ascension Day. These days had a character of their own because they were holidays at a pleasant time of the year, yet also days of penitence when lay people joined the clergy in great walking processions. In Exeter, this involved going from the cathedral through the streets and into the fields. 'Today and on the three days following', says one of the exercises, 'people go in procession round the towns and fields with relics, crosses, and banners, singing the litany and praying for the peace and prosperity of the Church.' The processions seem to have made for an outlying chapel where, at the normal time for dinner (eleven o'clock), mass was celebrated and a sermon was preached, after which the hungry crowds partook of special food.

As these days were penitential, it was not proper to eat meat. On the other hand, unlike Lent, dairy products were allowed. It seems therefore to have been the custom to celebrate Rogationtide with tempting dishes like flans which did not contain meat. The cathedral spent £1 or £2 a year on flour, eggs, cheese, butter, cream, saffron, and honey to make large flans for its staff and perhaps for guests. The school exercises allude to this practice. 'The foods which I ate on the last Rogation days were onions and leeks with butter, and also creamed milk, junket, and flans.' The writer goes on to point out that he does not love fish on these occasions except for dainty ones:

'lampreys, eels, loaches, coleys, milts, turbots, trout, plaices, porpoises, crabs, lobsters, and salmon.' Rogationtide was a popular festival – it survived the Reformation – and it looks as though part of the popularity came from the consumption of these tasty snacks of sea-food, dairy products, and choice vegetables.

It did not take long to walk into the countryside; the city contained only a few thousand people and scarcely stretched beyond the ancient walls. 'Of all the fields in which I have walked', says one passage, 'the most beautiful lie around this town: verdant with plants and grasses and dressed with lovely flowers.' Inside the walls, people were busy with making and selling cloth: one passage boasts that you can wear a gown which has been spun, woven, fulled, and dyed in the city. Exeter had its own mayor and council, and the exercises mention the annual election of the mayor by the leading inhabitants, followed by a distribution of pears as a refreshment. Every so often, the king's

A fifteenth-century schoolmaster and his class

judges arrived to hold the assizes, and the mayor gave orders that extra food and horse fodder should be made available for them and the barristers who came with them.

The school knew about other places too. York was three times greater than Exeter, and London three times superior to York. London had the king's court at Westminster, accurately described as lying on the west side of the city and the north bank of the Thames. The exercises also refer to Pontefract, the university towns of Oxford and Cambridge, and their counterparts in France: Paris and Orleans. Three passages mention royal courtiers or servants, with evident disapproval. 'At night in the twilight while we were going home to supper, we directed two men of the court on horseback; they looked like thieves.' Another 'thief of the court' is described as having 'clothes of the new fashion and hair hanging like a cloak from the loins to the shoulders, turned up like a duck's tail'. 'Some who are dressed like courtiers', observes a third exercise, 'are more fitted to rob than to do any good service to their masters.' At this time court fashion was changing from the short hair-cuts of Henry V's time to a liking for very long hair – a change apparently disliked by the clerical schoolmaster.

This period was one when Henry VI's court was becoming unpopular for its alleged corruption. The year 1450 saw the rising of Jack Cade in Kent and the murder of the king's chief minister, the duke of Suffolk. A poet and school-founder who married Chaucer's grand-daughter, he was accused of having lost the war with France. In 1452 Henry was obliged to visit Exeter as part of his attempt to restore confidence in his government, and may be to this event that the courtier references belong. There were other local annoyances in Exeter, although they were not the fault of Henry VI and his court but older and longer-lasting problems. Doors needed to be shut for fear of thieves, eliciting the view that 'thieves who rob the good and just of their property deserve to perish by hanging'. Personal violence was common. The writer of the exercises considered that long hair put a man at the mercy of an adversary quite unnecessarily, and one passage tells or imagines how the writer's enemy lay in wait for him in the dark and was put to flight with a sword.

Disease was another concern. We learn that children have been much afflicted by scurfs, poxes, and pustules. Seers foretell from this that a pestilence will soon appear, although it is observed that such people are often wrong. News comes that pestilence has broken out at Oxford. 'The scholars are leaving and fleeing, hurrying home each to his own birthplace, to stay there until the outbreak has subsided'. It was common for schools and universities in this period to close when epidemics came, and this may have happened from time to time in Exeter. In 1536, the cathedral sent the choristers home to escape a raging 'pestilential plague'.[4]

And all the while, because we are in Devon, the winds blew and the rain came down. During the winter, tempests raged so much that people blamed the fact on necromancers calling up spirits to look for mines of gold and silver. Then as now, science was held responsible for the weather. Rain fell for three months and springs bubbled up on the hills and in the houses, until even the elderly said that such things had never been known. Matters grew better with the coming of spring. 'The day grows more and the morning longer, with a clear and bright light'. The school looked forward to the coming of the cuckoo and the burgeoning of plants and herbs. But the weather in Devon is rarely settled. In May or June, the rain fell copiously for a week, together with strong winds and tempests. How comforting it was, the writer thought, to live in a well-tiled house where you could keep yourself and your clothes dry. Wind, weather, truancy, thieves, and unpopular ministers – it is remarkable how much has remained the same!

9 WARS AND WONDERS

The night has been unruly. Where we lay,
Our chimneys were blown down, and, as they say,
Lamentings heard i' th' air, strange screams of death.
                              William Shakespeare, Macbeth

The writing of history in the middle ages prompts the thought of a monk in a cloister inscribing a Latin chronicle. Such writing was sometimes done, and one or two leading monasteries, notably St Albans and Westminster, took it seriously, but it was not much practised at cathedrals like Exeter. Cathedral clergy spent their time on worship and administration rather than on literary compositions. They might read chronicles for pleasure, but they rarely wrote them. John of Salisbury and Adam Murimuth, two well-known medieval historians, were canons of Exeter in the late twelfth and early fourteenth centuries respectively, but their histories belong to their careers elsewhere. Devon (then as now) was remote from national affairs. When, in about 1300, someone at Exeter compiled a Latin chronicle, it was short enough to be displayed on a board inside the cathedral and it centred on the history of the building and the reigns of the bishops, not on events outside.[1]

There are, however, some more humble signs of interest in historical events among the cathedral clergy. They survive in the beautifully decorated thirteenth-century psalter, still preserved in the cathedral library, which originally belonged (it seems) to a church in Worcester and passed from there to Exeter at an early date.[2] The first few leaves of the psalter contain a calendar listing the days of each month and the feasts of the major saints that fell upon them. In the fifteenth century, events began to be noted in this calendar: at first towards the bottom of the pages but later, with more boldness, against the days of the months themselves.[3] There are thirteen of these notes, the earliest referring to the year 1431 and the last to 1547. They were written by more than one person and represent people's wishes to record unusual happenings on an occasional, rather than a regular, basis.

We have some grounds for guessing who made the notes from our knowledge of the role of this particular psalter in the cathedral's life and work. In 1506 it was stated to belong to the second form of the choir: the middle rank of the seating which was occupied by the secondaries (the twelve adolescent clergy) and the annuellars.[4] The psalter was used by one or other of these groups, and as the second form contained another copy given by a former annuellar, the one we are dealing with may well have been special to the secondaries. Two other features possibly point to them too. First, the notes are all in Latin, of a kind that was written in schools. Some of the secondaries attended the High School, and the notes accord with the kind of Latin one would expect its scholars to write. Secondly, the fact that the notes are about unusual and striking events may indicate younger people who found news exciting, rather than older clergy who had seen it all before.

The events fall into three categories: unusual natural phenomena, political happenings, and religious executions. Few phenomena of the skies inspire such awe as comets, and our ancestors were impressed by them even more than we are:

On the first day of this month [January] in the year of the Lord 1471, a certain star appeared amazingly in this region, in the south east of the sky: not shining luminously within itself but like a pot of fiery radiance, emitting a long hair-like ray in the manner of a great flame of fire, telling the hearts of

The Exeter clock, showing the world at the centre of the universe. The moon and sun revolve round it, marking the days and the hours

those who observed it that the misfortune of the terrible thing would bring about disasters, which may the Lord turn into joy for us! Amen.

Comets were believed to foreshadow calamities. A London citizen, who noted the star of 1471 and called it *stella comata*, asserted that its appearance was followed by 'great mortality and death of people through the land, with many other inconveniences'.[5] When another such star appeared at Exeter in Henry VIII's reign, it too was feared to be the herald of troubles:

> On 9 August in the year of the Lord 1521 a comet was seen in various places in the west and in the northern region, in the likeness of a flaming fire, emitting fiery rays on high. May God be favourable!

This was an age that thought of the universe as a huge machine, directed by God, with the world at its centre. The main dial of the cathedral clock still represents this view. When unusual signs appeared in the heavens, God not only caused them but meant them to have an impact on the world. They were his warnings that punishments or afflictions were about to descend on mankind.

The other great natural event described in the psalter is the storm of 1467. Here the writer can be left to tell his own story. First comes a Latin verse couplet:

> *Ecce tonat Bricius et mactat vulnere gentes,*
> *An[no] semel m, c quater, semel l, ter et v, bis adest i.*
> (Hark on St Brice's Day, thunder, striking to injure the people!
> Year of one thousand, four hundred, fifty, three fives, and two others.)

Then follows a passage of Latin prose:

> On St Brice's Day [13 November] 1467, and in the seventh year of the reign of King Edward IV, a most violent north-westerly wind suddenly developed

throughout the whole kingdom, lasting for thirty-six hours and more: overthrowing bell-towers and pinnacles, rolling up the lead on holy places and elsewhere, sadly sinking five ships supported by their anchors and many others laden on the high seas elsewhere, memorably taking away great oaks and elsewhere fruit trees of various species, demolishing houses and walls, wonderfully and violently picking up the tiles from some of them. People were so demoralised that they would scarcely go out of their dwellings or, alternatively, stay inside them any longer. The merciful Lord, who stirred this up because of our demerit, finally abating it, may he be blessed! Amen.[6]

These entries do not tell us anything very particular about the storm in Exeter, but they are interesting nonetheless. Like the passages about the comets, they resemble the kind of Latin learnt in grammar schools like the Exeter High School which we encountered in the previous chapter.[7] The presence of these passages in the psalter reinforces the impression that the book was used by young men still at school, or recently out of it, who were used to writing this kind of commentary on the news. As in the High School exercises, the Latin is strong on vocabulary, using a wide range of words, and weak on style, which is rather clumsy and over-ambitious. It gives a valuable insight into the literary skills and knowledge of men who were employed at the cathedral and would become priests in the Church, if they had not already done so.

The largest number of entries in the psalter relate to political events, and they are shorter than the passages encountered so far. Most of them fall between 1471 and 1513, which is probably not accidental since this was a period when Exeter was more than usually involved with national politics. The first such entry, noted on 15 April but correctly belonging to the 14th, is

The battle near Barnet, in the year of the Lord 1471, on Easter Day, to which someone else has added *vbi lacrimosa clades erat* ('where there was a sad disaster'). The Wars of the Roses had begun in 1455 and Barnet, one of the closing battles, saw King Edward IV and the Yorkists gain a decisive victory over the Lancastrian supporters of Henry VI.

Barnet would have been of special interest for Exonians because its two main protagonists – Edward IV and Warwick the Kingmaker – had both visited Exeter in the previous year.[8] Warwick had ridden through quickly in flight from Edward, and the king, failing to catch him, had lingered for a while in the city and worshipped at the cathedral. Later, Warwick recovered the upper hand and Edward was forced into exile. The Lancastrian queen, Margaret of Anjou, and her son Edward Prince of Wales came over from France to help Warwick, and they too passed through Exeter in April 1471. Local people had therefore seen the major actors in this phase of the Wars of the Roses, and must have been especially curious about the outcome. Some may have favoured Margaret and Warwick – the earl of Devon, John Courtenay, was a staunch Lancastrian – and the additional note seems to express a regret about the outcome of the battle. Warwick was killed and the Lancastrian cause was badly damaged. Edward then turned west to deal with Margaret and the Prince of Wales. He met and defeated them at Tewkesbury, and this battle is also recorded in the psalter:

> 4 May. Here was the battle at Tewkesbury, in the year of the Lord 1471, where many of the noble race were killed.

Tewkesbury was famous for its casualties. The prince was slain, probably in the battle, along with the earl of Devon and other leading Lancastrian supporters. After the battle Edward IV executed many of his prisoners, achieving final victory over his enemies.

The next political entries relate to the events of 1497 – a year which affected Exeter even more greatly than 1471.[9] In the autumn of 1496 the king of Scots, James IV, raided the north of England on behalf of Perkin Warbeck, the pretender who claimed to be the younger son of Edward IV. Henry VII, now king of England, secured a grant of heavy taxation from Parliament to finance the defence of the north, and this sparked off a rebellion in Cornwall. In May 1497 the Cornish marched to London to protest, passing by Exeter where (we are told) the mayor was obliged to allow the leaders and their retinues to march through the city while the rank and file went round the outside. Local people must have been agog to know what would happen to the Cornish, and in due course the news came:

> 17 June. The battle at Blackheath was fought in the year of the Lord 1497.

The Cornish were routed and their leaders executed. But Blackheath was not the end of the affair, for James IV next provided Perkin Warbeck with a ship and supplies to cause trouble in southern England.

On 7 September Perkin disembarked near Land's End and gathered a second force of Cornish, arriving with them at Exeter on Sunday 17 September. The city's defenders (led by the earl of Devon) refused him entry and, as the note-maker put it,

> Note that on St Lambert's Day [17 September], the fourth [correctly the fifteenth] before the kalends of October, there was the battle at the gates of Exeter between the [knights?] of Devon and Perkin Warbeck, in the thirteenth year of the reign of our king Henry VII.

The ill-equipped Cornish failed to storm the city and suffered heavy losses, partly from the city's guns. They broke off the engagement and marched on to Taunton, where Perkin fled and his army disbanded. Then it was Henry VII's turn. He arrived in Devon to settle the region and,

> On the morrow of St Faith the Virgin, that is to say 7 October in the year of the Lord 1497, our most excellent king Henry VII entered Exeter.

He gave the city, as a mark of his favour, the cap and sword which it still possesses, and pardoned some of the rebels in the cathedral close itself. Henry experienced no more trouble from the South West, but the affair had a sequel in an entry of sixteen years later:

> On the ninth day of the month of September in the year of the Lord 1513 the king of Scotland, James by name, was killed at Branxton.

This was at the battle now usually known as Flodden. James, one suspects, would have been remembered in Exeter as the king whose actions had caused the troubles of 1497. Now he had been trounced in the worst defeat of the Scots in all their wars with England, and lay dead on the field along with two abbots, three bishops, and twelve of his earls. His meddling in English affairs had been well and truly avenged.

The last category of entries in the psalter concerns religious executions. These were rare events in Exeter and must, especially for clergy, have been of startling interest:

> On 10 January in the year of the Lord 1531, according to the course and computation of the Church of England [i.e. 1532, modern style], Thomas Benet [here two or three words have been erased] was burnt at Livery Dole.

Benet's execution touched the cathedral closely. He had posted up a bill on one of its doors in the previous October, attacking the pope and the worship of the saints. The Reformation began in Germany in 1517, but England at this time was still Catholic and most of the Exeter clergy were strong traditionalists. Benet kept a private school in South Street and, when he unwisely sent one of his boys to stick up a second bill, the lad was caught and Benet was traced. Tried for heresy, he might have escaped the death penalty by recanting his beliefs but refused to do so and was burnt at Livery Dole, the local place for hanging criminals. Benet's fate would have been impressive because it was so unusual in Devon, and it happened only once more in the sixteenth century when Agnes Prest from Cornwall was burnt in Southernhay in 1558.[10] In 1909 a martyrs' memorial to Benet and Prest was erected on the corner of Barnfield Road and Denmark Road, and still stands there.

The psalter shows, however, that Thomas and Agnes were not the first people to suffer death for religion in Exeter. The earliest of all the notes is this:

> On St Donatus's Day in the year of the Lord 1431, that is to say 7 August, Drew Steyner [two or three words have been rubbed out] was deservedly burnt at Livery Dole.

The note refers either to a man whose Christian name was Drew and whose surname was Steyner, or to someone surnamed Drew and employed as a 'stainer' or painter of fabrics. I have found no other evidence about him in any records, but there is no reason to doubt the truth of the entry. Ever since the 1380s England had had a home-grown heresy, Lollardy, based on the teachings of John Wycliffe, and this had been preached in the South West of England at an early date by Laurence Bedeman, one of Wycliffe's Oxford disciples. No other Lollards are recorded in Devon until the early sixteenth century, but that does not mean that they did not exist: they may have kept their heads down and the authorities have left them alone.

In 1431, however, the forces of law and order were more vigilant than usual. Some Lollards were extremists interested in fomenting political disorder and one of them, William Perkins, tried to organise a rising in Berkshire and Wiltshire in May of that year. Perkins was caught and executed, other suspects were pursued or dealt with, and Drew Steyner may have been one of them – unless he was a harmless local man caught up in the repression. Heresy was such a comparatively rare crime and so serious – it could lead to death after 1401 – that suspected heretics were usually tried by the bishop himself. The bishop of Exeter in 1431 was Edmund Lacy whose register of acts survives, but curiously it contains no entries between March and late

September that year. This stops us checking whether the bishop was involved, but equally leaves open the possibility.

In the end, those who had been condemned as heretics became celebrated as martyrs. A little more than two years after Benet's execution the Church of England was separated from papal control and Henry VIII was declared its head. The psalter itself came into the hands of people who either supported the Reformation or did what it required them to do. Somebody carefully erased words about the two martyrs – words which probably described them as 'wicked heretics'. The calendar was altered to the political correctness of the late 1530s. Three entries relating to the feasts of St Thomas Becket were rubbed out, Henry VIII having suppressed his cult in 1538 because of his robust stance against an earlier King Henry. Saints who were popes, like Clement and Leo, had the word 'pope' removed from their titles, and the description of St Anne as 'mother of St Mary' was also effaced. The last entry was made in the calendar on 20 February:

> Here was crowned Edward VI in the year of the Lord 1546 [1547, modern style].

Under Edward, changes more radical than those of Henry VIII were made to the cathedral's worship, staff and furniture – changes of lasting effect. They also affected the psalter, which ceased to be used. No further notes were made in it and it was tidied away to the cathedral library. We are lucky that it has survived, and with it these bits of what was once the breaking news of the day.

10 A VISITOR IN 1478

> I met a traveller from an antique land.
> *Percy Bysshe Shelley, 'Ozymandias'*

On a September day in 1478, a traveller left the Bear Inn in South Street (where the church of the Sacred Heart stands nowadays) and walked up the adjoining lane, under the Bear Gate, into the precincts of Exeter Cathedral. He had been born in the year of Agincourt and, at sixty-three, was elderly by the standards of his day, but he was still athletic and was riding home on a journey which took him 800 miles, mostly alone on horseback, over the space of two months. He was not a great man to his contemporaries. If so, he would have stayed with the cathedral clergy not at a public inn, but he is a great man to us. In his pocket that day he had some long narrow folded pieces of paper for making notes, and no doubt on his belt there hung a pen case and an inkhorn for writing. Of all the many visitors to Exeter Cathedral, he is the earliest who has left us a written account of what he did and saw, for his papers were kept when he died. Bound up into a notebook, they found their way into the library of Corpus Christi College, Cambridge, and rest there to this day.[1]

William Worcester, for that was his name, is one of the most interesting men of fifteenth-century England, and very different from the rash or devious warriors whom we associate with that age.[2] Born at Bristol in 1415, he studied at a local grammar school and at Oxford before entering not the Church but the service of the wealthy Norfolk landlord and war-veteran, Sir John Fastolf of Caister. Worcester became his secretary and man of business, helping to run the knight's estates, handle his legal affairs, and write his letters. When Fastolf died in 1459, leaving behind two wills and no family, Worcester (as an executor) became embroiled in fifteen years of litigation and disputes as various powerful people struggled to gain the inheritance.

Troubles now overtook him. He was arrested for debt, his property was seized, and his wife was put in prison in his stead. Yet throughout these difficulties, it was observed that he kept his humour and his interest in literature and history. For Worcester was a writer when chances allowed. He translated Cicero's *Old Age* into English, he wrote a *Book of Noblesse* defining the status and duties of noblemen, but most of all he was a pioneer of what we now call local history and archaeology. He observed and made notes on things around him: rivers and bridges, churches and monasteries, saints and shrines, trade and shipping, tombs and family history. He got some way towards completing an immensely detailed description of Bristol (which survives) and a history of the ancient families of East Anglia (which does not). Long before Leland, Norden, and the Tudor antiquarians, Worcester was measuring buildings, copying records, and plying the people he met with historical questions.

He did not come to the South West primarily to see Exeter Cathedral. Instead, like many modern travellers to Devon, his real objective was Cornwall. By 1478 Fastolf's affairs were settled, Worcester had gained possession of the property in Norfolk which Fastolf had promised him, and he could afford a holiday to do what he wanted. On 17 August he set out from Norwich on what was partly a pilgrimage to St Michael's Mount and partly a tour of places both familiar and new to him. He visited Salisbury, Bristol, Tintern, Glastonbury, Launceston, and Truro on the way down, and Exeter, Bath, and Winchester on the way back. Where possible he called at religious houses, looked at their calendars to find unusual saints and death dates of benefactors, and talked with the clergy about local history and topography. He had the gift of making instant friends: a groom of the king's at Truro, a notary in

Tavistock, a priest at Ottery St Mary, the abbot of Glastonbury at Westonzoyland. And he acquired and wrote down an extraordinary range of information: Cornish saints, the width of the English Channel, the birds of Gulland Rock, the course of the River Creedy, the islands of Wales. Historians used to be rather scornful of his jottings, mistaking them to be a finished work of poor quality. They are, in fact, just notes, but the notes of a keen observer with very wide interests.

We do not know exactly how long Worcester stayed in Exeter, but it was a matter of hours rather than days. He left Tavistock on the afternoon of Tuesday 22 September and probably spent the night at an inn at Okehampton or Crockernwell. He left Exeter on the following Thursday, not later than midday since he managed to get to Newenham Abbey near Axminster by evening, in spite of a stop for a drink and a talk at Ottery St Mary. He was only in Exeter for certain, therefore, from Wednesday afternoon to Thursday morning, and it is remarkable that he saw as much as he did in that time.

Like most visitors, he made his way to the cathedral and struck up a friendship with John Skinner whom he describes as 'subsexton of the doors' – perhaps a virger or assistant virger. He viewed the nave, the choir, and the transepts, and following his usual practice, measured them by pacing them out and noting the dimensions. Then he went into the cloisters which in those days formed a quadrangle around the cloister garth, calculated the length of the east side, and did the same in the chapter house where he saw the new east window built a few years earlier by Bishop Nevill.

In the cathedral itself, he observed that the clerestory windows each had five or six 'lights' or divisions and the aisle windows five. And he liked what he saw; he praised the design of the windows and declared that 'the whole church is vaulted over in a most beautiful way'. Two other features of the building caught his attention. One was the board displaying in Latin the major dates in the cathedral's history and the list of bishops – the earliest guide-book, as it were, for visitors. From this he noted that King Æthelstan was the first founder of the church, that Bishop Quinil began to build the present cathedral in 1288 (we now know that this happened earlier under Bronescombe), and that Bishop Lacy ruled from 1420 to 1455.

The other place that interested him was Lacy's tomb on the north side of the choir. Here he would have noticed candles burning, pilgrims at prayer, and wax images hung up as signs of cures required or received – images like those now kept in Exeter Museum. Stirred by his interest in saint cults, he copied down the first verse of a Latin sequence or prayer to the bishop, and the text of a Latin intercession recommended for pilgrims to use, in translation:

> Holy Edmund, goodly pastor,
> Clergy's father, loving master,
> Cleanse us now from our despair.
> From the dross of living take us,
> Be our help, and worthy make us
> Crowns in heaven at last to wear.

> Pray for us, blessed Edmund, that . . . [here you inserted your request].
> O God, who have made us glad by the merits and intercession of the blessed Edmund your confessor and bishop, mercifully grant that the benefits for which we ask may be obtained by the gift of your grace, through Christ our Lord. Amen.

These prayers must also have been posted up for the public to see, reminding us (like the board) that reading had become a central part of Church life even for lay people. We are a long way, by 1478, from the time when people depended for their understanding of religion on pictures and statues alone.

The 'beautiful vaulting' of the cathedral admired by William Worcester on his visit in 1478

Worcester did not restrict his movements to the cathedral. He had apparently met one of the canons, Dr Owen Lloyd, while travelling through Launceston, and they had discovered a common interest in Celtic matters. Lloyd, a Welshman, owned a copy of *The Itinerary through Wales* by Gerald of Wales, and must have invited Worcester to call in to see the book, since the Exeter section of Worcester's note-book contains two pages copied out of it.

From Lloyd's house in the close, Worcester went north-eastwards to the Dominican Friary (in what is now Bedford Street), probably in the hope of being shown the friary calendar and finding further saints and burials. He did not get to see it, but he met John Burges, one of the friars, and had a conversation which, to judge from Worcester's notes, went somewhat on these lines:

> *Burges*: What is your interest in calendars, Master William?
> *Worcester*: Saints, Master Friar, especially ones who are not widely known.
> *Burges*: By my faith, I can tell you some of those. There's Wulfric the priest –
> he lies in a church between Yeovil and Crewkerne, near your way back
> to London. There's St Brandwellan, a king's son and confessor – he lies
> at Branscombe.
> *Worcester*: Where's that?
> *Burges*: About eight miles from Axminster and four from the sea. Then
> there's St Sidwell the virgin – she lies in St Sidwell's church outside the
> East Gate [here Worcester wrote down 'east bridge' by mistake]. And
> then there's St Walter – his shrine is in the monastery at Cowick beyond
> the West Gate. He has been canonised, and the record of his life says that
> he was born in Norwich where you come from.

Tales heard by travellers are never wholly true. Burges was right about Wulfric and his shrine at Haselbury Plucknett in Somerset, but wrong about Branwalader who was honoured not at Branscombe (which seems to be named after a Brannoc) but at

Milton Abbey in Dorset. Burges's mileages are also decidedly shaky. It is a pity that he did not say, or Worcester did not tell us, more about St Walter of Cowick, Exeter's least-known saint, who probably lived in the late twelfth century. We know no more of Walter than that he visited purgatory (and returned!) and ever afterwards wore a goat skin, presumably as a penance.[3]

Did Worcester set out for Cowick to see Walter's shrine in the priory there? He certainly looked at the Exe Bridge, counted its sixteen arches, and reckoned its length as 200 of his steps, but that may have been before he talked to Burges. He did not get to Cowick, however, and the cloak of obscurity around Walter stays unlifted. Instead Worcester rode off to London on Thursday, his sheaf of notes a little thicker, never to return; he died some time between 1480 and 1485. His writings are not as coherent and will never be as famous as Boswell's *Tour to the Hebrides* or Cobbett's *Rural Rides* yet they possess the same haunting power to recreate the past. Reading them we travel the roads of fifteenth-century England with a genial companion: crossing rivers, admiring buildings, entering churches, and talking with people, as he did in that autumn long ago.

11 THE WITCH, THE CLOCK, AND THE BISHOP

King Richard: Well, but what's o'clock?
Buckingham: Upon the stroke of ten.
King Richard: Well, let it strike.
　　　William Shakespeare, Richard III

Bishop Hugh Oldham, who lies in the chapel of St Saviour at the east end of the cathedral, was the last bishop of Exeter to be buried in his own private enclosure within the cathedral. Anyone who visits this part of the church will see that St Saviour's chapel balances St George's at the other end of the aisle in front of the Lady Chapel. The two chapels were built in or shortly before 1513, one by Oldham and the other by Sir John Speke of White Lackington, Somerset, who died in 1518.[1] Both men were evidently friends. Oldham's coat of arms appears on the screen of Speke's chapel and their projects were planned as a single scheme. They were the only two major additions to the church after it was finished in the 1340s, and belong to the prosperous Indian summer which the cathedral enjoyed in the early sixteenth century, on the eve of the Reformation. Each founder endowed a priest to celebrate mass for his soul in his chapel every day for ever – a chantry priest in Speke's, a vicar choral in Oldham's. 'For ever' turned out to be only thirty years, however, since these kinds of masses were abolished in 1548–9.

Each chapel is like a jewel box, highly ornate inside and out, and repays careful study. They are full of religious statuary – saints and angels – some of which have lost their heads in the Reformation campaign against images. Speke and Oldham chose for their chapels religious dedications which were popular in the world outside. St George was the national saint of England; St Saviour was Our Saviour, Jesus Christ, thought of especially as the wounded Christ of the Cross.[2] A number of chapels of St Saviour were built in England up to the Reformation, particularly in or near ports like Bridgwater, Exmouth, Padstow, and Fowey in the West Country, where sailors or their passengers could pray for aid against peril before making a voyage. Inside the chapel, the honour given to Jesus is shared with his mother the Virgin Mary. On the stone reredos, the decorated backing of the altar, her figure dominates its left- and right-hand scenes which depict the Annunciation and the Nativity. She also seems to be portrayed outside by the door, sheltering her worshippers inside her cloak and crushing the serpent with her heel. This tendency to equalise the honour given to Mary with that accorded to Christ would, in a few years time, form something else to be attacked and adjusted by the Protestant Reformers.

In this respect, Oldham's chapel is still far away from the Reformation, but in another the shadow of that event already seems to fall over it. The chapel's imagery is markedly secular as well as religious. It is full of owls, one of which holds a label in its beak containing the letters DOM, 'Owldom', a rebus or pun on the bishop's name. There are shields with coats of arms: the diocese of Exeter, Bishop Oldham's own arms, and one which apparently joins the arms of King Æthelstan (who refounded the Anglo-Saxon minster at Exeter) and King Edward the Confessor (who made it into a cathedral). And over and above this is the presence of the king of the day: Henry VII who promoted Oldham to power or Henry VIII who succeeded him in 1509. Everywhere we see the Tudor symbols: the large rose, the portcullis, the royal coat of arms, and its supporters the greyhound and the dragon. Even the letter H which is so widely displayed, could stand as well for Henry as for Hugh. In short, Oldham and Speke, unlike earlier bishops such as Grandisson or Lacy, wished or felt obliged to show their respect for their ruler. Their chapels proclaimed not only their own importance and that of their favourite saints but that of the Crown. It was this aura of monarchy and the willingness of bishops and knights to bow before it which explains why Henry VIII and his successors were able to carry out the Reformation with so little opposition.

Exeter's bishops have fallen into two main sorts: scholars and administrators. Hugh Oldham belonged to the latter kind.[3] He was born near Manchester into a family of minor gentry, and his first known job, in 1478, was that of a clerk in the king's chancery. By 1492 he had become the receiver in charge of the West Country estates of Lady Margaret Beaufort, mother of Henry VII, and rose in her favour to become chancellor of her household. He studied arts and law at Oxford – it is not clear when – and in 1492 he took a degree in law at Cambridge. He became bishop of Exeter in 1504, a reward interpreted (probably rightly) as due to his patroness, and he ruled the diocese for fourteen and a half years. Lady Margaret was the centre of a group of people interested in promoting education. She herself founded chairs of divinity at Oxford and Cambridge and two colleges in the latter, and Hugh shared her interests.

As bishop of Exeter he was careful to ensure that the men he ordained were properly examined. Those he appointed as cathedral clergy and diocesan administrators were generally university graduates. In 1511 he laid down that the secondaries – the adolescent clerks of the cathedral choir – should attend the city High School, and during the 1510s he took a leading part in establishing Manchester Grammar School, which still survives, to provide free education in Latin grammar for the countryside where he originated. He also played an important part in the foundation of Corpus Christi College, Oxford. At home, he was a friend of the cathedral. In 1509 he suppressed two decaying local hospitals, Clyst Gabriel at Bishop's Clyst and Warland at Totnes, and transferred their revenues to the vicars choral. This allowed the vicars to have regular meals together in their common hall in Kalendarhay, in the manner of a university college.[4]

Hugh Oldham is unusual for his time because we possess some stories about him collected by the Exeter historian John Hooker (*c.*1526–1601), who grew up among men who still remembered him. Hooker wrote down these stories in three places: his *Catalog* or history of the bishops of Exeter which he published in 1584, his edition of Raphael Holinshed's *Chronicles of England* which came out in 1587, and his unpublished annals of the city of Exeter.[5] Oldham left a reputation as a man with a gruff exterior but a kind heart. 'He was', writes Hooker, 'a man having more zeal than knowledge and more devotion than learning; somewhat rough in speech but friendly in doings', although in another place Hooker describes him simply as 'surly'.[6] He was punctilious in his daily life and 'very precise to keep his profixed and accustomed hours [for meals], namely at eleven of the clock for his dinner and five of the clock for his supper'.

People in those days got up earlier than we do and had their meals sooner. To

Bishop Oldham on his tomb in St Saviour's chapel

make sure that his meals were served on time, Oldham kept a clock in his house with a servant to look after it, but this caused difficulties. The bishop expected the clock to strike the time for dinner or supper only when he was ready to eat, so the clock-keeper delayed the clock from striking until that happened. People in the household would ask what time it was, and the keeper would say 'as it pleases my lord'. The bishop himself would sometimes enquire the time and receive the same answer, 'as pleaseth your lordship, if you be ready to go to dinner, the clock will be eleven'!

Hooker also heard stories about Oldham's attempt to found a university college. 'He first was minded to have enlarged Exeter College [the main college with west-of-England links] in Oxford, as well in buildings as in fellowships. But after being a requester to the fellows for one Atkins to be a fellow, in whose favour he had written his letters and was denied, he changed his mind and his good will was alienated.'[7] Next he thought of helping with the foundation of Brasenose College, which had recently been established by his friend William Smith, bishop of Lincoln, but being refused the title of co-founder, he backed away. Finally, he came to a satisfactory arrangement with another friend, Richard Fox, bishop of Winchester, who was engaged in founding Corpus Christi College. Oldham gave Corpus Christi £4,000 and lands in Chelsea, in return for which the college recognised him as a benefactor, prayed for him every day, and undertook to admit one scholar and one fellow from Oldham's home county of Lancashire.

Fox's first plan for Corpus Christi, drafted in 1513, was for a mixed college of eight monks from Winchester Cathedral (then a monastery) and an unspecified number of 'secular', meaning non-monastic, students. By the time that the college statues were issued in 1517, the plan omitted the monks – a change which Exeter gossip attributed to Oldham.[8] Hooker represents Oldham as saying to Fox that 'monks were but a sort of buzzing flies, and whose state could not long endure', or as it is put in another version of the story, 'What, my lord! shall we build houses and provide livelihoods for a company of buzzing monks, whose end and fall we ourselves may live to see?

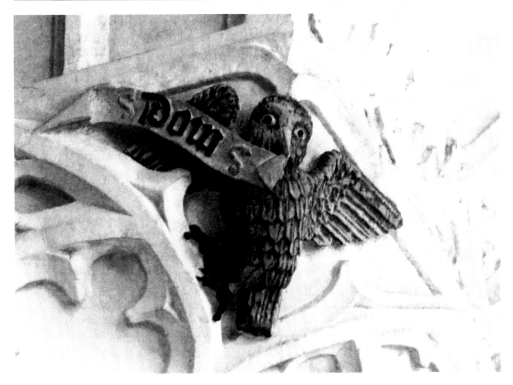

*Bishop Oldham's
'Owl-dom' rebus in
St Saviour's Chapel*

No, no! It is more meet a great deal that we should have care to provide for the increase of learning and for such as who by their learning shall do good in the Church and commonwealth.'

One suspects that Hooker, no friend of monks and writing after the Reformation, exaggerated Oldham's foresight about the fall of the monasteries, which was not at all obvious in the 1510s. Indeed Oldham, despite a long dispute with Tavistock

Abbey while he was bishop, does not seem to have been unfriendly towards monks. He involved the abbot of Whalley in the foundation of Manchester Grammar School and was willing to be buried in an abbey if he chanced to die near one.[9]

Hooker's other stories relate to Oldham's death in 1519. When the bishop was gravely ill, he was advised to seek the help of a woman from Crediton whom he had tried for witchcraft in a 'very hard and extreme' way. The bishop held out for some time but at last he yielded, and the witch, with equal reluctance, was persuaded to visit him. After some preliminaries, the witch told the bishop to repeat after her, 'Hugh Oldham, by thy full name, aryse up yn Goddes name!' He did and lo! he sat up in bed. Then the witch said, 'and lie thou downe agayn yn the devells name'! He sank back, 'and never recovered nor yet rose out of his bed after'. The witch existed and her name was Alice Waren. We know that she got into trouble with Oldham and that after his death, 'having been persuaded by the devil to return to her wickedness', she was summoned to appear before Bishop Veysey in 1524.[10] If she visited Oldham, she did so in the summer of 1519, for he died on 25 June and was buried in his chapel.

There was a story about that, too. As a result of his litigation with the abbot of Tavistock, the bishop, says Hooker, was excommunicated by the papal court 'and could not be suffered to be buried until an absolution from Rome was procured for him'. This seems an unlikely penalty for a well-connected bishop who named as his executors Bishop Fox, the dean, the subdean, and the suffragan bishop, but it shows, like the episode of the witch, that Oldham's reputation gave rise to stories of 'the biter bit' variety. He was remembered as a hard man whose hardness sometimes injured himself. We can certainly dismiss an elaboration of this story which circulated in Exeter by the eighteenth century, that the excommunicated bishop had to be buried outside the cathedral – hence the building of his chapel for the purpose.[11] The chapel existed six years before the bishop's death, and the bishop was buried, as he intended, in the splendid setting that he had planned for himself.

12 BREAK, BREAK, BREAK

My aspens dear, whose airy cages quelled,
Quelled or quenched in leaves the leaping sun,
All felled, felled, are all felled.
                    Gerard Manley Hopkins, 'Binsey Poplars'

Walking through Exeter Cathedral today, you are likely to be impressed by its order and completeness. Not much appears to be awry inside, broken or ruined, apart from the inevitable wear and tear of time. The screen between the nave and the choir stands up impressively with its carvings, paintings, and the great organ case above it. The east end of the choir looks neat, with the pillar and open arches behind the high altar. The building and its contents seem to have weathered the political and religious upheavals of the past in such a wonderful way that what we see today is not very different from what our ancestors would have seen five hundred years ago.

This view of the past is understandable but it is mistaken. Between 1538 and 1660 the cathedral underwent many alterations: not to improve its colour and decoration but to reduce them. Up to the 1530s the cathedral was lovingly filled with art: stained-glass windows, altar coverings, vestments, paintings, sculptures, tombs, and monumental brasses. Then there was a sudden change of mind, and most of these things were damaged or removed. The change was due to the Reformation which, in England, involved a great deal of iconoclasm – hostility to images, not only of saints but of Christ, the Trinity, and sometimes even effigies on tombs. This hostility emerged quite early in the Reformation, under Henry VIII who is often supposed to have been conservative in many of his religious sympathies. He was not in this case.

In 1538 Thomas Lord Cromwell, Henry's chief minister and deputy ruler of the Church of England, issued injunctions to the English clergy in the king's name forbidding the worship of images. No one was to venerate a statue or painting of God or the saints by praying before it or making a pilgrimage to it. Images might remain as reminders of Christianity, but any that were venerated should be removed. The king's government was not content with mere instructions, either. It organised the destruction of relics and images, sometimes in public. The most notorious of these was the 'Holy Rood of Boxley', a large statue of Christ on the Cross at Boxley Abbey in Kent. When it was taken down, wires and rods were found inside that could move the eyes and the lips, as if the Christ was miraculously alive. The image was taken to London, shown to the king and the court, and exhibited at a public sermon by the bishop of Rochester. He accused the monks of Boxley of duping the people, and told his listeners that all images should be taken away to prevent idolatry. The sermon ended with the breaking of the Rood into pieces.[1]

The destruction of images in Exeter began at about the same time. The leading spirit in the process was the new cathedral dean, Simon Heynes, who had been appointed by Henry VIII in the previous year, 1537. Heynes was a strong, indeed a radical, supporter of the king and the Reformation, and thereby differed greatly from the rest of the cathedral clergy whose sympathies were Catholic and conservative. Their sympathies would have been well known in London, and Heynes may have been deliberately appointed to counteract them. He was unpopular from the moment of his arrival: an outsider from Cambridge University whereas most of the canons were from Oxford, and a known supporter of change. He behaved in a high-handed manner too, demanding greater powers and perquisites than previous deans had enjoyed. And he made it a priority to enforce the injunctions of 1538 in the cathedral.

We do not know exactly when or in what order he did so, but one of his earliest targets must have been the tomb of Bishop Lacy in the north choir aisle. This tomb was still an object of veneration; as recently as 1534 a Somerset clergyman had left money in his will for someone to go 'to Bishop Lacy' and offer twenty pence at his tomb.[2] Visitors came in search of relief from ailments to the limbs, ailments that the bishop had suffered himself and which (it was believed) he could cure or could ask God to cure. The pilgrims hung up little wax models on strings around the tomb: models that they could probably buy in the cathedral. These represented fingers, feet, legs, horses' legs, and even whole human bodies, which people wanted cured or displayed as a sign of thanks when they were cured. By 1542 when the Tudor traveller John Leland visited the cathedral, Heynes had caused the brass image of the bishop to be ripped from the tomb,[3] and the wax models may have been cleared away at the same time. A cache of them was found in 1942, hidden upon the screen above the tomb, perhaps in the hope that Heynes and his reforms would be reversed one day.[4]

The cathedral clergy later complained that Heynes had done much damage without consulting them. He had destroyed several beautiful images, although they had not been objects of superstition. He had injured the cathedral walls and flooring. He had lacerated books in the choir, causing damage valued at over £13. This would have involved striking out references to the pope and to Thomas Becket, a saint detested by the Reformers because he stood up for the privileges of the Church against a previous King Henry. Heynes had taken away the perpetual light on the high altar, although the king's laws had not forbidden it.[5] We hear from a different source that he removed a large figure of Christ that hung on an outside wall of St Mary Major, the parish church that used to stand a little way west of the cathedral. This figure was venerated by local people, and there are mentions in cathedral records of sums of money being offered to it.[6]

Heynes's actions were only the first of a series. During the reign of Edward VI (1547–1553) nearly all the images of saints were removed from the cathedral. The

The damaged reredos in St Saviour's chapel. Left, the Annunciation; centre, the Mass of St Gregory; right, the Nativity

great crucifix on the choir screen was taken down, and so were the statues of the Virgin Mary, St Peter, and St Paul which stood by the high altar, and those of saints like John the Baptist and Katherine by the lesser altars in the cathedral chapels. Behind the high altar there was, up to this time, a great stone screen elaborately decorated with ornate pinnacles not unlike the sedilia that still survive in the south-east corner of the choir. The stone screen had stone images of saints in niches, and these were all removed. Eventually the screen was reduced to a plain flat wall. In 1550 stone altars were forbidden. The high altar was demolished and replaced by a wooden table, and the other altars were dismantled as well.

Under Elizabeth I (1558–1603) even the tomb of Bishop Grandisson was thrown out of his chapel in the thickness of the wall between the nave and the west front of the cathedral. This tomb would not have been venerated, and the only reason one can imagine for removing it was that the chapel (no longer used for worship) was wanted for storage. By this time there was little reverence even for tombs, so that monumental brasses, for example, were often pulled off their stones simply for the sake of their value as scrap metal. The last phase of iconoclasm happened as late as the 1640s and 50s, when Puritans hostile to images were briefly in power and the cathedral was famously divided into two churches for their use.

One of the casualties of the Reformation was the stone reredos or little screen behind the altar in Bishop Oldham's chapel of St Saviour. It still survives in the chapel in a damaged state, allowing us both a rare glimpse of what Catholic art in the cathedral was like and how the Reformers reacted against it. The damage cannot be dated exactly, but the period from 1538 to 1553 is very likely because one of the panels on the reredos would have been especially obnoxious to Heynes and like-minded people during this period. The reredos has in fact three panels on it. To the left is the Annunciation of Gabriel to the Virgin Mary, and to the right the Nativity of Christ. Between them is the 'Mass of St Gregory' or 'Pity of St Gregory' as it used to be called.

This central panel illustrates a popular legend about St Gregory the Great, the pope who sent St Augustine to bring Christianity to the English. One day Gregory was celebrating mass; you can just make out part of him, kneeling in front of an altar. Around him are some of his cardinals, two on each side. A chalice lies on the altar, which he has just consecrated. Suddenly a vision of Christ appears behind the altar: an almost naked Christ displaying his wounds as he did on the Cross, but standing resurrected on his tomb. The tomb, like an oblong coffin, can be seen but the figure of Christ has been almost obliterated. Behind the tomb is the Cross, and on the left of it, are the spears that were used to offer Christ a sponge soaked in vinegar and to pierce his side to test if he was dead. On the right is the ladder used for taking him down from the Cross.

Pictures of this legend were very popular in the middle ages. They were painted on walls, carved as images, and illustrated in prayer books and as cheap block prints on paper or parchment. Christians prayed to the image in church or in their homes; indeed, if you look at the effigy of Bishop Oldham in the chapel, you will see that his face and body are turned in such a way that he is doing so, even in death. Those who prayed in this way were believed to earn indulgences – remission of the penances due for their sins – and by the early sixteenth century the indulgences were claimed as granting the worshipper the huge amount of 32,755 years of remission.[7] This explains why the English Reformers disliked the image so much and worked so hard to spoil or erase it. Indulgences were closely linked with the claims of the popes to be able to forgive sins and penances, and it was impossible to leave the image intact because it would continue to remind people of the pope and his claims. People might go on venerating the image silently and believing that they were gaining the indulgences.

The Pity of St Gregory had another obnoxious feature, especially after 1547 when the Reformation became overtly Protestant. It expressed the Catholic doctrine about the celebration of the mass or Eucharist. This doctrine held that, when the priest

consecrated the bread and the wine in the service, their substances were turned or 'transubstantiated' into the real body and blood of Christ. Gregory's vision seemed to prove this doctrine. As soon as he consecrated the bread and wine, Christ appeared at once in bodily form. Paintings and prints of the scene often showed blood falling from Christ's wounds into the chalice, and this may have been portrayed in some way on Oldham's reredos. But the doctrine of transubstantiation was anathema to Protestants, who argued that the bread and wine of the mass, or holy communion as they called it, was a reminder of Christ's last supper or underwent at most a spiritual transformation not a physical one.

So the Reformers had particular reasons to hate the Mass of St Gregory, and they defaced it in Oldham's chapel. Yet significantly, they defaced it rather than removing it. It is as if they wanted to say 'This is the superstition that people once believed. We have destroyed it.' The solution was a neat one. An image that was originally meant to encourage Catholic piety was changed into one that proclaimed the triumph of the Reformation. It still speaks of the passions of that time.

13 TAKEN TO THE TOWER

Well have you argued, sir, and for your pains,
Of capital treason we arrest you here.
William Shakespeare, Richard II

There was a good deal of rejoicing when Mary Tudor became queen of England in 1553 – not least in Devon and Cornwall. Only four years earlier, the region had seen the great 'Prayer Book Rebellion' against Cranmer's *Book of Common Prayer* and other Reformation changes. Now, the old religious order was to be re-established. The queen and her advisors, including Reginald Pole, the new archbishop of Canterbury, had to find religious leaders to rebuild Catholicism after thirteen years of Henry VIII's Church of England and six more years of Edward VI's Protestant version. Who was the man entrusted with this task in Exeter, the last Roman Catholic bishop?

Mary's first action was to turn out Edward's bishop, the Bible translator Miles Coverdale, and to replace him with his predecessor, John Veysey, a Catholic sympathiser who had been removed from office in 1551. Veysey was a very elderly man by this time, aged about ninety and living in retirement at Sutton Coldfield. Nonetheless he answered the call to duty. He came to Exeter in November 1553, and stayed there for nearly two months before returning to Sutton. Under him, the Latin Catholic services were restored in the parishes, and clergy who had taken advantage of Edward's permission to marry were summarily ejected from their benefices. Veysey, however, died on the night of 22/23 October 1554, and the Crown had to find a replacement. After some delay it fixed on James Turberville, canon of Chichester and Winchester Cathedrals. He was nominated as bishop of Exeter by the Crown on 11 March 1555, granted custody of the lands and revenues of the see on 6 May, 'provided' by the pope (the technical term for appointment) in September, and consecrated in St Paul's Cathedral on or about the 8th of that month.

Turberville was sixty years old in 1555 and had not played a prominent role in the Church under Henry VIII or Edward VI. But Mary and her Catholic archbishop of Canterbury, Cardinal Pole, did not have a wide choice of men to be bishops. Nearly every cleric in England had outwardly accepted Henry's brand of Anglicanism and Edward's Protestant Church. They were conformers, not enthusiasts. In Turberville's favour, he had not been actively involved with the Reformation and he had two other solid advantages by Tudor standards. He was well born and well educated. His father, John Turberville, had been lord of the manor of Bere Regis, Dorset, sometimes sheriff of Somerset and Dorset, and a member of a long-established family of gentry.

James himself was born in 1494. He entered Winchester College as a scholar in 1507, aged twelve, and went on to New College Oxford in 1512. He became a fellow of the college and took the degrees of BA in 1516 and MA in 1520. During the early 1520s he learned administrative skills. He acted as a scribe for the university and as a notary public. In 1525 he was ordained priest, and went abroad to study theology – we do not know where. By 1531 he was a doctor of divinity, and in 1532 the University of Oxford 'incorporated' him to the same degree. Meanwhile, he had resigned his college fellowship and acquired a series of church benefices. He became, among other things, rector of Over Moigne and Lytchett Matravers, Dorset, rector of Hartfield, Sussex, as well as holding his canonries at Chichester and Winchester.[1]

These facts read like an entry in Crockford's *Clerical Directory*, and give us no sense of Turberville as a person. Here, unfortunately, our sources are poor. Each bishop of Exeter kept registers of his activities, and we possess two of Turberville's, one listing the clergy he ordained and admitted to Church benefices, and another recording his 'common' or miscellaneous business. Neither register, however, contains much information and none of a personal nature. Even his movements in his diocese are unknown, and virtually nothing can be said about his role in the restoration of Catholicism. Some of his parishes returned to the old religion with enthusiasm. At Morebath, high up on the edge of Exmoor, the vicar, Christopher Trychay, noted with satisfaction how local people brought out the images and ornaments which they had hidden in Edward's reign:

> Of John Williams of Berry we received again an image of Mary . . . And of William Morsse at Lawton was received an image of John, and of the Widow Jurdyn trails and knots. And of diverse other persons here was received pages and books and diverse other things concerning our rood loft. Like true and faithful Christian people this was restored to the church, by the which doings it showeth that they did like good Catholic men.[2]

Other parishes, some more slowly or less willingly, restored their altars and images too. It would be good to know what happened in the cathedral, but its records in the 1550s are disappointing. We are told only that a Dutchman was employed to repair the faces of the images damaged under Edward VI. These must have been stone images forming part of the building; the old wooden moveable ones had probably been destroyed altogether.[3]

The harm done to Catholicism by the Reformation made its restoration a task of great difficulty. The bishop himself was now less powerful. Henry and Edward had taken much of his property in Devon. His residence in London, Exeter House in the Strand, had passed to William Lord Paget. The parish churches had lost their old prayer books and vestments, as well as their altars and images, involving time and expense in acquiring new ones. The religious guilds which had done so much to support Church worship had been abolished, and it was hard to revive them. Everyone had become familiar with Protestantism. There had been English Bibles in churches since 1539 and English services since 1549. Many people preferred the new religion and, while not openly challenging the new Catholic order, remained disaffected in private. In the end, the crucial factor for Catholicism was lack of time. Queen Mary reigned for only five and a half years, and Turberville was bishop of Exeter for scarcely more than three.

Our sole surviving assessment of his character and personality comes from his contemporary, the historian John Hooker, chamberlain of the city of Exeter. Hooker was a Protestant who had no liking for Catholics, but his two short appraisals of Turberville are fair and neutral. In his *Catalog of the Bishops of Exeter*, published in 1584, he says that

> He was a gentleman born, and of a
> good house, very gentle and courteous.

The bishop's throne where Turberville once sat

He professed divinity, but [was] most zealous in the Romish religion, and yet nothing cruel nor bloody. And yet, that he might not seem to do nothing, he was contented to prosecute and condemn a guiltless poor silly woman, named Agnes Priest, for religion and heresy, and who was burnt in Southernhay for the same.

In his manuscript 'Annals of Exeter', Hooker also uses the words 'mild, courteous, and gentle' but qualifies this slightly: 'not so forward in bloody matters [meaning persecutions] as he had officers to follow it'. In other words, Turberville got others to do his dirty work. His main achievement, in Hooker's eyes, was to regain some of the bishop's forfeited property. In 1556 the Crown leased back to him the valuable estate at Crediton, lost by Bishop Veysey under Henry VIII, and he subsequently rented out part of this to his nephew Nicholas. But by the time that Hooker was writing, what Turberville recovered had largely been lost again.[4]

The greatest blot on the bishop's reputation, in Hooker's view, was the affair of Agnes Priest or Prest. Agnes, a woman in her fifties from Boyton near Launceston, had picked up Protestant views from hearing sermons, presumably during Edward's reign. This caused her to fall out with her husband and children and to leave them, supporting herself by her skill at spinning. She was eventually reported to the authorities for heresy, and put into Launceston gaol. Later she was brought to Exeter for investigation by the clergy. There is a detailed history of her case in John Foxe's famous *Book of Martyrs*, who says that he based it on information from people present. He gives a circumstantial account of her examination by the bishop, to whom she proclaimed her disbelief in the Catholic doctrine of the Eucharist and her conviction that all images were idols. Subsequently she declared the pope to be Antichrist. Turberville's replies to her contain no traces of his reputed courtesy and mildness, but that is not surprising since Foxe was a fierce opponent of Catholics. He or his informants present the bishop as speaking condescendingly and irascibly, scolding Agnes as an unlearned woman for presuming to hold views of her own on serious religious matters.

Turberville's initial decision was to send Agnes to his prison. He hoped that his clergy would convince her to submit to the Church, and for a time even this imprisonment was only a nominal one. She was allowed to live in the gaoler's house, doing servant work and continuing with her spinning. She had freedom to walk about in the city and managed to meet some local people who sympathised with her views. But after a month or so, when she remained firm in her beliefs, she was subjected to stricter confinement, convicted of heresy, and finally handed over to the secular authorities. She was burnt in Southernhay by the sheriff of Devon in August 1558. By our standards, the treatment of her was repugnant. By theirs, they handled her with some tolerance, probably because they regarded her as ignorant and eccentric. Her experience hardly suggests that the bishop was active in looking for heretics, and she was the only person to suffer death for religious views during Turberville's time in office – a very different story from London, where many Protestants were burnt.[5]

When Queen Mary died on 17 November 1558, it soon became apparent that the Church would move back in a Protestant direction under her sister, Elizabeth I. In the spring of 1559, the Crown introduced laws into Parliament to re-establish the Church of England. What were the bishops to do? They had all done what they were told by the three previous monarchs, but most of them balked at accepting Protestantism again after five years enforcing Catholicism. They voted against the new legislation, and when they were ordered to take an oath to recognise the queen as the supreme governor of all things religious and temporal, all but one refused, including Turberville.

The chapter of Exeter Cathedral was divided on how to react. Some followed the bishops, including the dean, Thomas Reynolds, whom Mary had meant to be bishop of Hereford; John Blaxton, the treasurer and president of the bishop's court; and apparently John Pollard, the archdeacon of Totnes, and Thomas Nutcombe, the subdean. All lost their offices. The rest of their colleagues took the oath and stayed: the precentor, Richard Petre; the chancellor, William Leveson; and the archdeacons of Exeter (George Carew), Cornwall (George Harvey), and Barnstaple (Henry Squire). Leveson was an old survivor, a nephew of Bishop Veysey, who had served under all the regimes since 1537, but the other four had been appointed during Mary's reign. Their willingness to comply shows that she had not succeeded in stiffening their loyalty, let alone that of the rank and file clergy in the parishes.

By the late summer of 1559 the English government had decided that the bishops, if they would not conform, must be removed from power. Turberville was accordingly deprived of his bishopric on 10 August, but the fact that no successor was appointed for several months suggests that the government hoped to win him over. In the end, all the bishops stayed resolute, except for Anthony Kitchin of Llandaff. In May 1560 steps were taken to appoint a new bishop of Exeter, William Alley, and on 18 June Turberville was sent to the Tower of London, along with most of his episcopal colleagues. Their imprisonment was relatively mild, and by September they were permitted to eat together. Turberville was released from the Tower on 6 September 1563, after intercessions by the Emperor Ferdinand, and transferred to the custody of Edmund Grindal, bishop of London. Some two years later, Grindal applied to the Privy Council for permission to let his prisoner go, and on 30 January 1565 the Privy Council agreed to this, on condition that Turberville remained in London and made himself available when required.

His freedom did not last for long. Later that year the government re-arrested the Catholic bishops and put them back in the Tower.[6] They were simply too dangerous to remain at large as potential leaders of Catholics, many of whom lived in London, and the suggestions by some writers that Turberville retired to the West Country or was even buried in Exeter Cathedral are wide of the mark.[7] He died in 1570, almost certainly still in the Tower. His place of burial is unknown and no monument is recorded in his memory. In that respect he has been less fortunate than Agnes, who is remembered on the Exeter martyrs' memorial in Denmark Road.

14 FROM EXETER TO LONDON IN 1562

Boot, saddle, to horse, and away!
Robert Browning, 'Cavalier Tunes'

On Saturday 18 April 1562, when Elizabeth I was twenty-nine and had been queen for three years, a little group of horsemen clattered out of the cathedral close at Exeter, at about the hour of noon. Their leader, Canon William Marwood, was travelling on business to London, and as befitted the wealthy cathedral clergy of his day he was accompanied by two men–servants of his household, riding on geldings from his own stable.

The canon himself was a man of about forty-five, unmarried like most clergy at that time, for clerical marriage had been allowed only recently. He bore the surname of a well-known family of gentry in north Devon, but he himself seems to have been connected with Modbury on the southern edge of the county. He made his way to Oxford University, graduated as a master of arts, and eventually in 1552 (when he was in his mid-thirties) became rector of Dunchideock. By 1562 he had also acquired the rectories of Tedburn St Mary and Torbrian in Devon, a canonry of Exeter Cathedral, and one of Salisbury too, ending up as a prosperous clerical pluralist with an income of over £100 a year. As he resided at Exeter for most of the time, he could not serve his country parishes in person, but even if he paid curates to do so (as he should have done), he still had enough wealth to live in a comfortable style.[1]

There were many travellers between Exeter and London in the sixteenth century, and William Marwood stands out from the others only because he kept a record of his journeys: one in April and another in the autumn of 1562. The record survives as a booklet in the cathedral archives consisting of eight paper leaves bound in a parchment cover made out of a discarded legal document.[2] On the cover are inscribed the words *Compotus Willelmi Marwod* ('The Account of William Marwood') and the contents state, in diary form, the days on which he travelled, the places he visited, and the money he expended on the way. William kept this record because he was carrying out official business for the dean and chapter, and was going to have his expenses refunded. In 1562 he had only been a canon of Exeter for two years, and his employment on the cathedral's affairs tells us something about his character and reputation.

William seems to have been a natural administrator rather than a scholar or evangelist. Some notes about the Exeter canons written in 1561 say that he was 'sufficiently learned' but not a graduate or a preacher, and although the second of these remarks is inaccurate, it does not suggest that his academic or pastoral qualities were very obvious.[3] He specialised in Church law and finance. He acted as 'surrogate' or deputy to the commissary general, the presiding officer of the bishop's consistory court which dealt with religious and moral crimes and the probate of wills. His journeys to London were concerned with fairly complicated financial business. It is probable that his benefices and the money they brought him were rewards for making himself useful in such matters to the bishop, the dean and chapter, and other important people.

The mission which took him from Exeter in 1562 was concerned with the payment of taxation by the clergy of Devon and Cornwall. Four years previously, when Philip and Mary were on the throne, the English clergy (who still granted taxation to the Crown in their own convocation, independently of Parliament) had agreed to pay a 'subsidy' of a tenth of their incomes every year on Lady Day for the next four years.[4]

The money was to be collected by the bishops or, if any bishopric were vacant, by the local dean and chapter. After Queen Mary died in 1558, most of the bishops, like James Turberville, stayed loyal to the Catholic faith and were deprived of their sees. Turberville was removed in about August 1559 and the bishopric then lay vacant until William Alley was nominated in the spring of 1560, which made the dean and chapter responsible for collecting the third instalment of the subsidy due in March of that year. The last portion was paid in 1561, and the following twelve months were designated for settling the accounts and making up any deficit, hence William's two expeditions to London. The dean and chapter were allowed to deduct 6d. in the pound for expenses from what they collected, so they could afford to cover William's costs on the journeys. Not that these costs were cheap, for his total claim amounted to nearly £25: enough in those days to pay three country curates for a whole year.

The clerical subsidy of 1558–61 has long been gathered and spent, but William's claim for expenses still has a value as a record of daily life in Elizabethan England. During 1562 the canon and his men travelled the roads between Exeter and London four times, starting out on 18 April, coming back on 16 May, repeating the outward journey on 25 September, and returning again on 11 November. The time spent on each journey varied from 4½ to 5½ days, of which between 4 and 4½ were passed in travelling, half a day being always taken up by resting, delays, or business on the way. This represented moderately fast, comfortable travel: slower than messengers or postmen, but quicker than carriers or carters. The route to London followed the modern A30 save for a deviation from Salisbury to Andover, rejoining the main road at Basingstoke. On both the journeys up, the party left Exeter at midday and rode 17 miles to Honiton where they had supper and spent the night.

The second day saw them covering 14 miles in the morning, eating (midday) dinner at Chard, and going another 22 miles in the afternoon, reaching Sherborne for supper and bed. On the third day they travelled 16 miles to Shaftesbury for dinner, and spent the rest of the day there, supping and sleeping as well. The halt may have been for the riders' benefit or that of the horses, one of which (as we shall see) went lame at about this point. The fourth day took them 38 miles through Salisbury to Andover for dinner, and another 19 to Basingstoke for supper, a total of 57, the longest daily ride. On the fifth day they covered 19 miles to Bagshot for dinner and 16 to Hounslow for supper, leaving themselves an easy 12 miles on the morning of the sixth day to reach London, where they arrived by dinner time.

The canon and his men thus rode for anything between 12 and 38 miles in the morning (the average working out as 22), and 14 to 29 in the afternoon (with an average of 20). Altogether, riders at this speed could expect to cover about 42 miles a day, barring bad weather or accidents to the horses, but Canon Marwood was not greatly concerned about haste: in both the spring and autumn he left the direct route to visit Windsor. When the riders stopped to rest at midday or the evening they had a meal, probably at an inn, for which they were charged anything from 1s. 6d. to 3s. 4d. for the three of them, whether it was for dinner or supper. Drinking in the morning, corresponding to our breakfast, cost about 4d. or 6d.

Curiously, Marwood's account does not include expenses for accommodation, although its mentions of drinking and (in the autumn) fires suggest that the party usually stayed the night at inns. So either beds were free, or he paid for them himself, or he and his men dossed down in their clothes. Once or twice they received hospitality on the road: at Windsor where they were asked out to dinner and at Salisbury where they spent a night at the house of Marwood's 'farmer', the agent whom he employed to collect his revenues as canon. Here they were entertained for nothing, but the canon distributed 1s. 4d. in tips. All the payments are meticulously recorded, and there is no indication that the canon fiddled his claims in an improper way.

The men's expenses were equalled by those of their horses. 'Horsemeat' (meaning fodder) for the canon's geldings cost from 1s. 4d. to 1s. 8d. for the three at midday,

*Canons' houses such as
William Marwood lived
in. Their medieval fabric
often survives behind the
later frontages*

when the animals had a lighter meal, and from 2s. 8d. to 4s. 8d. in the evening when they were given more. When Marwood was in London, they were boarded in livery stables and, not being worked, were cheaper to feed, their food then costing only 1s. 2d. a day (8s. 6d. a week). There were other expenses than food. The horses were re-shod in Exeter before each journey up, costing 3s. 4d. for the three (or just over 3d. a hoof), but this did not suffice for the round trip and further shoeing was necessary on both occasions: 2s. 8d. worth at Salisbury in May, and an unspecified sum there in November. Mending a saddle at Windsor cost 6d. Worse still, a horse might suffer injury or sickness. One of the canon's geldings fell lame near Shaftesbury on the first journey up in April and had to be treated by the earl of Pembroke's farrier in Salisbury, who dressed the injury at a charge of 5s. Later, 8d. was spent in London on oil of bay, a substance often used in the sixteenth century for lame or injured steeds. The second journey up was more troublesome than the first in this respect. 'Horses' in the plural needed attention at Shaftesbury, costing 3s. 4d. for dressing them there. By Basingstoke one horse had grown too lame to ride, so an extra mount had to be hired for 20s. for the rest of the journey, as well as costing extra for its food. Then the horses fell sick, apparently while Marwood was in London, and 8s. 4d. was expended 'for dressing my horse legs and tongue and drenching of them and for the farrier's attendance'. Finally, the lame horse gave trouble again on the way home, requiring 4s. worth of shoeing and dressing in Salisbury; a last 4d. was spent on a shoe in Yeovil. Horse travel seems romantic nowadays; Marwood's experiences show how tiresome it could be.

William stayed in London for two and a half weeks from April to May and five weeks from September to November. We do not know where he lived, and as he noted only his official expenses (food, fires, candles, and washing), we do not hear of visits, shopping, or amusements. There would have been ample time for all these, since the subsidy proved to be a complex matter, taking weeks to finalise. The problem centred on a recent revaluation of the English currency. During the 1540s and 50s the governments of Henry VIII and Edward VI had debased the coinage in order to raise revenue, and coins were issued containing less gold and silver than they were nominally worth. In September 1560 Elizabeth's regime decided to restore the currency to a higher standard, and a royal proclamation ordered that the base coins should lose a quarter or more of their face value and be returned to the mint.[5]

Many of the Exeter clergy must have paid the subsidy of March 1560 in base coin – a good way of disposing of it! – and because they paid up late or the collectors were slow to forward the money, the payments had not been completed when the September proclamation caused their value to drop. The government then demanded extra to make up the loss. William Marwood went to see the lord treasurer (the marquess of Winchester) on 1 October to discuss the matter, giving a shilling to the usher who let him into the marquess's presence, but the government would not abate its claim and the officers of the royal exchequer decided that Exeter should pay a further £156. William had to find this money at once, which he did by borrowing it from a merchant and two Tiverton clothiers who were staying in London. What with other delays, it was not until 27 October that he was able to hand over the final instalment to the exchequer, receiving a receipt in the form of a written 'bill' and a wooden tally (and he was charged 1s. 10d. even for this). He stayed for one more week, and then went home with the London part of the business settled.

William Marwood lived for another 19 years, and the last we hear of him is his will, dated 20 August 1581 and proved (after his death) on 6 September.[6] Like the account book, it reveals the comfortable life-style of an Exeter canon in the reign of Elizabeth I, with its mentions of William's clock and 'all my books', clothes including his best cap, two cloth gowns and one of worsted, feather-beds, bolsters, pillows, sheets, and blankets. The canon had half a dozen servants, including a cook, and seems to have kept up the rector's house at Dunchideock as well as his canonical residence at Exeter. He also gave alms on the scale expected of men of his rank: 20s. to the poor of each of his three parishes, 40s. to those of Modbury where he was probably born, 1s. 8d. to every man and woman in an almshouse in Exeter, and 13s. 4d. to the inmates of the two city prisons. He never married, and bequeathed his property to his brother, sister, nephews, nieces, and his friend Robert Harcourt. William did not specify where he wished to be buried and he has no known grave, so the little book in the archives is his chief memorial. We can be grateful for its glimpses of the ways he rode and the problems he encountered long ago.

15 BETJEMAN AND EXETER

'Come all to church, good people' –
Oh, noisy bells, be dumb;
I hear you, I will come.
           A. E. Housman, 'Bredon Hill'

Exeter is not very rich in associations with national poets. Chaucer, perhaps, passed through on his visit to Dartmouth in 1373, and Shakespeare mentions the city briefly in *Richard III.* He tells the story, which came from John Hooker of Exeter, about how Richard was shown the castle in 1483 and started when he was told the name of it, 'Rougemont',

Because a bard of Ireland told me once
I should not live long after I saw Richmond![1]

The city was the birthplace of two minor poets, Durfey and Baring-Gould, and Hardy wrote two poems about it, both in a sombre vein. In 'A Cathedral Façade at Midnight', he watched the light play on the statues of the west front and reflected on the decline of faith. In 'The Carrier', which is set in Sidwell Street, he told of the driver who kept a vacant place beside him in his van, where his dead wife used to sit.[2] But the list of Exeter poems and poets is not a long one, and the late Sir John Betjeman's contribution, 'Exeter', is consequently a welcome addition.

The poem in question was written in the mid-1930s. In 1934 Betjeman produced a motorist's guide-book to Cornwall: *Cornwall Illustrated in a Series of Views*. This was the first of what became the 'Shell Guides' to the English countryside, financed by the petrol company. After completing Cornwall, Betjeman started on Devon. The Devon guide appeared in 1936, so the work was presumably done in that and the previous year. In writing the Shell guides, Betjeman aimed at producing a new kind of guide-book. First, it should be amusing as well as informative, varying facts with humorous comments and plenty of pictures. Secondly, it was to cast its net wider than the standard guide-book fare (cathedrals, castles, and half-timbered houses) to cover buildings of the eighteenth and nineteenth centuries (churches, chapels, and streets) which were usually ignored by tourists and those who wrote for them. As the Shell guides were short, not much could be said about any one place, but an exception was made for Exeter and Betjeman gave it three pages, including several photographs.[3] In general, he liked the city:

> It is the first town to give the traveller from London a feeling that he is in Devon. Honiton is grey and elmy; Exeter is mellow red with here and there ilex-trees and sandstone church towers and stately terraces.

His analysis, on the other hand, was highly original for its time. Previous guide-books to Exeter had generally concentrated on the cathedral close and the picturesque buildings in the High Street. The cathedral in particular was treated with awe and veneration. Betjeman felt that the cathedral, although interesting, was only one in a city of many beautiful buildings, and he set out with panache to cut it down to size:

> People go to Exeter, park their cars in the close, look at the Cathedral, and conclude that they have "done" Exeter. To my mind the Cathedral is the most disappointing thing about Exeter. Its west front is singularly ill-proportioned, and the really vile Victorian church of St Mary Major close beside it [now

demolished] does not add to the harmony of the scene. . . . The most impressive things about the exterior of the Cathedral are the great black Norman towers at the transepts and the green clipped grass of the close.

Inside, he found some features to approve:

The interior, which is made mysterious by the well-placed organ case, is mostly in the Decorated style of Gothic architecture and mostly 14th-cent. work. The effect is one of extreme richness and elaboration. The interior is squatter than most cathedrals and on a different plan.

He duly mentions the minstrels' gallery, clock, throne, and east window. But even here, his use of the word 'squat' and his likening of the bishop's throne (which takes to pieces) to a child's construction toy, brought a new and, one must say, a fresher approach to the subject, compared with the hallowed tones of earlier writers.

Having blown raspberries at the cathedral, Betjeman went on to devote the majority of his article to less familiar places, particularly those out of the city centre. He praised the church of St David's, lamented the impending destruction of St Paul's, and liked the 'quaint' part of the city in the West Quarter, 'where the houses tumble down towards the beautiful Custom House':

But the most beautiful parts of Exeter have still to be seen. They are easily reached by leaving the close at the east side under a delicate iron bridge (1814) and going into Southernhaye (1800–16). On a sunny day these mellow brick houses, with their delicate iron-work, white woodwork, and handsome doors, look beautiful framed by the olive ilex-trees in the square.

This area of the city, with its Georgian buildings, filled him with delight. Southernhay (as we now spell it) had 'a Methodist chapel of beauty' and 'the handsome hospital'. Colleton Crescent was 'as good as anything in Bath except the Royal Crescent'. Nobody ought to miss Barnfield Crescent, and the fact that one's first view of it was spoilt by 'a modern house in the Golder's Green half-timber style' struck him merely as comic. He even put in a photograph to show the incongruous result. He was impressed by the Lower and Higher Markets, 'designed by a genius called Fowler', and altogether concluded that 'Exeter repays a day of exploration'. It is clear that he felt that most of this day should be spent in the Georgian streets rather than around the cathedral, and his photographs tried to lure the tourist in that direction. Four were devoted to Georgian splendours, and only one to the cathedral. Typically he chose a print of 'the well-placed organ case'.

The poem 'Exeter' was an imaginative complement to the guide. It was evidently written during his visit to Exeter or soon afterwards, and was published in his second volume of verse, *Continual Dew*, in 1937. In the Shell guide, Betjeman had referred to Southernhay as a place 'where doctors and

The screen and organ, interrupting the view and luring the visitor eastwards

solicitors live in Georgian calm'. In the poem, he imagined the life of one of the doctors' wives. When asked by me if the poem was based on real events, Betjeman wrote in a letter of 1981 that it was not: it was an imaginary story, suggested by the character of Exeter's Georgian streets. The poem describes the doctor's wife who used to go regularly to cathedral services. But her faith weakens or disappears, which is symbolised by her reading one of Aldous Huxley's risqué novels—possibly *Brave New World* which was published in 1933. When her husband is killed in a car-accident, the experience leads her back to the Church.

The poem shares several features with the guide: the pink or red of the city's buildings, the ilex-trees, the cathedral, and two of the streets. And just as the guide plays off the cathedral against the Georgian areas, so does the poem, the contrast between the two being one of its themes. Although there are topographical references in the poem, the topography is rather vague. We are not told where the doctor's wife lived, only that the cathedral bells called her 'through Southernhaye'; you might think from the poem that she lived in Colleton Crescent, whereas Betjeman associated the doctors with Southernhay, not the Crescent. The street names, clearly, are not included for accuracy but to suggest associations: mellow brick walls and quiet streets.

The puzzling reference to 'Wilfric's altar' is also inaccurate. It is probably a misremembered form of Leofric, the first bishop of Exeter. Betjeman studied Anglo-Saxon at Oxford but hated its names and words, and never bothered with them afterwards. He meant the cathedral high altar. The music of Stanford, on the other hand, was certainly popular at the cathedral, and the A service was performed six times in 1935, including Easter Sunday.[4] When 'Exeter' was reprinted in Betjeman's *Collected Poems* in 1958, the words 'through Southernhaye' were changed to 'to praise and pray', and 'Wilfric' became 'Wulfric'. It is a pity that the changes took away part of the local setting of the poem, while failing to correct the mistake about Leofric.

As a poem, 'Exeter' has something in common with Houseman's lyric 'Bredon Hill'. Both tell of a similar sequence of events, beginning in summer. Religious duty is forgotten – in Housman's case through falling in love – and the characters stay away from church despite the calling of the bells. Tragedy intervenes, one partner dies, and the other obeys the bells and returns to church. The difference lies in the setting. Housman's Bredon is ageless: hill, thyme, larks, and the view of the coloured counties. Betjeman's poem has ageless elements, faith and death, but they are set alongside the minutiae of everyday life in the 1930s. He had already explored the incongruousness with which great happenings take place in ordinary surroundings, in his first good published poem 'Death in Leamington'. He was to do the same in several later poems, notably 'In a Bath Tea Shop'.

In 'Exeter' loss of faith goes hand-in-hand with Aldous Huxley, of all people, and death with *The Sketch* and *The Tatler* – society magazines that featured the activities of (among other people) Mr and Mrs John Betjeman! This technique gives a fresh insight into tragic or comic events, and is, of course, a hallmark of Betjeman's work. His best poems feature not only a great event but a period setting, and blend the two together with striking effect. It is appropriate that his literary achievements were recognised in Exeter in 1971, when the university gave him an honorary degree.

The text of the poem which follows is the original one of 1937. It is reprinted by kind permission of the late Sir John Betjeman and of his publishers, Messrs John Murray.

EXETER

The doctor's intellectual wife
Sat under the ilex tree
The Cathedral bells pealed over the wall
But never a bell heard she
And the sun played shadowgraphs on her book
Which was writ by A. Huxléy.

Once those bells, those Exeter bells
Called her through Southernhaye
By pink, acacia-shaded walls
Several times a day
To Wilfric's altar and riddel posts
While the choir sang STANFORD IN A.

The doctor jumps in his Morris car—
The surgery door goes bang,
Clash and whirr down Colleton Crescent,
Other cars all go hang
My little bus is enough for us—
Till a tram car bell went clang.

They brought him in by the big front door
And a smiling corpse was he;
On the dining-room table they laid him out
Where the BYSTANDERS used to be—
THE TATLER, THE SKETCH and THE BYSTANDER
For the canons' wives to see.

Now those bells, those Exeter bells
Call her through Southernhaye
By pink, acacia-shaded walls
Several times a day
To Wilfric's altar and riddel posts
And the choir sings STANFORD IN A.

16 'AM IN ILFRACOMBE: WHY?'

He thought he saw an Elephant,
That practised on a fife;
He looked again, and found it was
A letter from his wife.
'At length I realize,' he said,
'The bitterness of life'.
Lewis Carroll, Sylvia and Bruno

High on the bishop's throne of the cathedral stands St Peter: bearded, holding a pastoral staff, and blessing those beneath him. Another bearded saint, this time St Martin, appears on the west end of the screen of the Speke chapel, giving his cloak to a beggar. Both sculptures were put into the cathedral in or shortly after 1936, and both were modelled on a real bishop of Exeter: Lord William Rupert Ernest Gascoyne-Cecil, who died in the summer of that year. The figures of St Martin and the beggar were given by the Mothers' Union of Exeter diocese – appropriately for a man well known for his interest both in mothers and in tramps. On the floor by the bishop's throne, a tablet expresses the wish that the figure of St Peter will 'keep for ever alive the memory' of Lord William Cecil.[1]

Such a wish still hardly seems required. Lord William's own personality has ensured, more effectively than any tablet or statues, that he lives in popular memory. And few

Lord William Cecil as St Martin, taking the begger's cloak in mistake for his own

indeed are the men and women (however famous in their lifetimes) who achieve remembrance in that way. 'He was', said the writer of his *Times* obituary, putting the matter delicately, 'a man of great originality of thought, whose logical processes did not show sign of early mental discipline'.[2] We shall return to this point presently, but let us first remind ourselves of his life. He was born in 1863, the fourth child and third son of Lord Robert Gascoyne-Cecil, later third marquess of Salisbury and four times prime minister of Great Britain. The family was a talented one, and William's brothers – the fourth marquess, Lord Hugh, and Lord Robert – all became active politicians.

William went to Eton and then to University College (Oxford), where his name already appears mis-spelt in the *Oxford University Calendar* as 'Gascoyn Cecil'. He took a third-class degree in law and decided to enter the Church. Fortunately for him, his family had ample means to support him in this vocation. In 1888, after spending a year as a curate in Great Yarmouth, he was presented by his father to the wealthy rectory of Bishop's Hatfield, Hertfordshire, when he was only twenty-five. There he spent the next 28 years with his wife, Lady Florence Mary Bootle-Wilbraham, daughter of the earl of Lathom, in a long and successful marriage that eventually produced four sons and three daughters.

The parish of Bishop's Hatfield contained the Cecils' family seat of Hatfield House as well as the market town of Hatfield with a population (in those days) of over four thousand. The Cecils took religion seriously, and Lord William had the help of a quartet of curates. He became rural dean of Hertford and an honorary canon of St Albans Cathedral, and it was these responsibilities – according to one reckoning – that gave him a claim to be promoted in the Church. A different opinion alleges that the Cecil family became tired of William's disorganised sermons ('they gave the impression of a certain raggedness', as *The Times* expressed it) and sought to find him a niche elsewhere in some cathedral canonry.

Later folklore tells how Lord William's brother, the fourth marquess of Salisbury, suggested to the prime minister (Mr Asquith) that William needed a change, and was amazed to learn soon afterwards that he was to be appointed bishop of Exeter. Mr Asquith, however, seems not to have acted solely out of kindness for William and his family. It was November 1916; the First World War was in progress, and Asquith's conduct of the war was coming under criticism. In December he was to resign. The Cecils were a leading Conservative family – Lord Robert was in the government – and Asquith needed to keep their loyalty. His offer of Exeter to William was later judged by *The Times* obituarist to have shown 'a fine disregard of political appropriateness'.

Appropriately or not, Lord William came to Exeter where his unusual demeanour soon became manifest. Disliking pomp, he refused to live in the bishop's palace and used it merely as an office. Instead, he bought a private house on the north side of Exeter, Barton Place – a dwelling which was not very much less grand. He did not succeed in permanently removing the bishop's residence from the palace (although his successor, Bishop Curzon, also lived elsewhere), but he did establish a new suffragan bishop of Plymouth at Tamerton Foliot in 1923 and had an idea (which never crystallised) of creating a separate diocese for the city. In his everyday work, he inherited the problem of Anglo-Catholic ritualism, especially in Plymouth – a problem which caused him less trouble than it had done his predecessors (although he too disliked it), because of the tendency of Anglo-Catholicism to become milder and more widely accepted. He also coincided with the development of ecumenism, which he endorsed sufficiently to preside at services involving members of the Free Churches.

His chief impact in the diocese, however, was as a personality rather than a leader. Bearded and unpredictable, he looked like a patriarch or prophet. At the same time, his aristocratic assurance led him to behave in an uninhibited and easy way with anyone he met, unlike middle-class bishops mindful of their dignity. In view of the comic stories to which Lord William has given rise, it would be only fair to recall that he had a large diocese to run and a number of tragedies in his family life. All but one of his sons were killed in the First World War, and one of his daughters died of a fever while young. He himself died in office on 23 June 1936, and was buried in the family church of Bishop's Hatfield.

We now leave history behind and move to the stories which have become attached to his name – doubtless often incorrectly because some are told about other people. I heard most of these stories in the 1960s and 70s from Francis George ('Frank') Rice, sometime prebendary, canon, and treasurer of Exeter Cathedral, who was born in Exeter in 1914 and lived and worked in the diocese for most of his life until he died in 1978. Frank was a thorough Devonian and, as chaplain to Bishop Robert Mortimer, had visited most corners of the county. He told these stories well, and writing them down fails to do justice to his warm chuckles and excellent sense of timing. He would interrupt me now and tell them better.

Frank's repertory included the two most famous William Cecil stories: the one about the telegram which his wife allegedly received, 'Am in Ilfracombe: Why?', and the other about the incident on the railway. In the second story, the bishop was travelling by train when he was asked to show his ticket. He searched his garments with mounting anxiety and lack of success, until the inspector said kindly, 'Don't worry, my lord. We know who you are.' 'That's all very well', said the bishop, frowning, 'but I need that ticket too. How else do I know where I'm going?'

The where and how of going places seem to have regularly caused him problems. He travelled each day from his house on the edge of Exeter to his office at the palace, and his preferred method of transport was a bicycle. In those halcyon days, you could leave your machine in the street and find it again when you wanted it or, in the bishop's case, find somebody else's and ride it home by mistake. Once he came back on a red bicycle belonging to a telegraph boy, and when his wife noticed this and sent him back to exchange it, he had to search for some time until he found the right house. The boy's mother was anxiously looking out, and he apologised handsomely and at length. Then he started to ride off, still on the same bicycle.

Lady Florence pondered this difficulty and hit on a clever solution: the purchase of a yellow bicycle, the only one in Exeter. Everyone else would know whose it was, even if the bishop did not. The bicycle was purchased and did indeed help to avoid mistakes, but Lord William remained prone to accidents. One day, the bicycle chain fell off and, despite the heroic efforts of the bishop's legs, the machine came to a standstill. A friendly passer-by offered assistance and refastened the chain, at some cost to the state of his hands, while the bishop offered profuse thanks and regrets at being a nuisance. 'Now', said Lord William, remounting, 'which way was I going?' When told, he pedalled away, remarking, 'Ah. That means I've had lunch.'

One day he attended a special service of the Mothers' Union in Plymouth. The preacher was a young clergyman who began his sermon with an arresting statement: 'Some of the happiest hours of my life have been spent in the arms of another man's wife'. The congregation was taken aback by this, but soon began to smile when the preacher continued, '. . . my mother!' The bishop was amused at the joke and stored it away in his memory. In due course, he was himself asked to preach at a Mothers'

Union service in Exeter, and decided to use the same opening. He entered the pulpit, invoked the Trinity, and the congregation sat down expectantly. 'Some of the happiest hours of my life have been spent in the arms of another man's wife.' There was a pause, a very long pause. The bishop ran his fingers through his beard. 'I'm sorry', he went on. 'I just can't remember her name.'

It was not only his own mother's identity; he was equally likely to forget the names or conditions of other people's mothers or wives. Attending a garden party at Buckingham Palace in the 1920s, he met a middle-aged gentleman with a distinguished air whom he thought he recognised. 'My dear sir,' he said, 'how very good to see you. How do you do?' The distinguished gentleman gave him a quizzical glance and answered rather shortly, 'Very well, thank you.' 'And your dear mother', continued the bishop, 'how is she?' At this, the middle-aged gentleman's face clouded. 'Why, she's dead, of course', he replied indignantly, and walked away. 'I didn't know that General Carslake's mother had died', said the bishop to his chaplain. 'Oh, that wasn't General Carslake, my lord', said the chaplain. 'That was His Royal Highness the Duke of Connaught.' The duke was the last surviving son of Queen Victoria and she, by then, had been dead for a quarter of a century.

A similar incident happened at Pinhoe parish fete near Exeter, but here the bishop was trumped by his victim, the vicar – the Reverend Oliver Puckridge, himself a whimsical character. While walking around the stalls, the bishop encountered the vicar and expressed his pleasure at meeting him. 'And how is your dear wife?' he added. 'I'm afraid she was taken from me last summer, my lord', said the vicar, and the bishop expressed his commiseration. They parted and the bishop resumed his walk, but half an hour later they met again. 'Ah, Mr Puckridge, how delightful to see you, and how is your dear wife?' 'Still dead, bishop. Still dead.'

The diocese of Exeter spreads far and wide, and out in the deep countryside live people who speak in strange dialects and call men 'to' not 'of' their addresses:

'Thomas to Satterleigh' and so on. Frank would tell a story about two farmers, somewhat the worse for drink, who drove away from the pub and took a wrong turning. 'I rackon we've got in the graveyard, Joe', said the driver. 'I can see a tombstone ahead. Miles to Crediton. Young chap he were, only 18.' Frank once accompanied another bishop, Robert Mortimer, to a country service at which a boy read the lesson with a broad accent. It was about the occasion when Jesus cured Peter's wife's mother of a fever. 'What is he saying?' asked Robert. Frank whispered loudly, 'He said he touched her for a fiver.'

Lord William also toured the remoter parts of his diocese, eventually acquiring a car for the purpose. Once, the episcopal automobile was stopped in a narrow lane by some sheep. The shepherd, passing by, touched his cap, and apologised. 'Oh, that's all right', replied the bishop, 'I'm a shepherd myself, you know.' 'Be you?' said the rustic, 'and where's your pasture then?' 'My flock covers the whole of Devon', said the bishop proudly, receiving the tart reply, 'Well, I don't know how you'll manage, come lambing time!'

A few weeks after one of Lord William's visits to the outback, the diocesan architect was asked to look at a problem affecting the roof of a church there. The farmer-churchwarden took him inside and led him up towards the high altar, where damp was coming through. In front of the altar were the usual altar rails, with a gap in the middle framed by two posts topped with large wooden balls. The architect rested his arm on one of the balls, at which the farmer interjected, 'Don't 'ee touch they balls!' 'Why not?' said the architect. 'They be holy balls', said the farmer. 'Bishop came here last month, confirming the children. As he went along the line, he did them too.'

Frank would often end his stories with the visit which Lord William was supposed to have made to a clergyman in some other outlying parish. The bishop was interested by the vicarage – an ancient building – and asked the incumbent if he found it comfortable. 'It's dreadfully cold, my lord', came the reply. 'In winter, we lie in bed for hours trying to get warm.' 'I do sympathise with you', said the bishop. 'My wife has the coldest feet of any woman I've ever slept with.'

Before luncheon, the bishop was invited to use the lavatory, which was inconveniently sited at one end of the house. He commented on the fact and turned his mind to how this might be improved. Indeed he interrupted the conversation several times to make suggestions about resiting the lavatory, only to be told that this or that possibility had been ruled out on grounds of space or plumbing.

The bishop concluded his visit and walked to his car. A number of parishioners had gathered outside the vicarage to see the great man depart, and the vicar (a High Church man) had warned them that Lord William might give an episcopal blessing. He had hinted to the bishop that they would like it, and had instructed them what to do in that event. Perhaps Lord William's dislike of ritual explains what happened next. As the bishop reached his car, he did indeed pause and raise his right arm. The vicar and the laity sank to their knees, joined their hands, and bowed their heads. But the bishop pointed back to the front of the house. 'Up there!' he cried, 'up there! Couldn't you put it up there?'

Now Lord William stands 'up there' himself, on the top of the bishop's throne. None of the stories about him may be absolutely truthful, but they witness to the remarkable impact he made. Not many bishops of Exeter since the Reformation have had two effigies erected in their memory, and none has gained such eminence in folklore.

FURTHER READING

A good deal has been written about the history of Exeter Cathedral in recent years, nearly all of it dealing with periods and topics before about 1550; more recent centuries are less well covered. The best general outline history and guide is by Vivian Hope, L. J. Lloyd, and Audrey M. Erskine, *Exeter Cathedral: a short history and description*, 2nd edn (Exeter, 1988). There is another fairly full account of the building in Bridget Cherry and Nikolaus Pevsner, *Devon* (The Buildings of England), 2nd edn (London, 1989). Two older books, George Oliver, *Lives of the Bishops of Exeter and a History of the Cathedral* (Exeter, 1861), and H. E. Bishop and E. K. Prideaux, *The Building of the Cathedral Church of St Peter in Exeter* (Exeter, 1922), still contain useful material but need correcting in certain respects.

The story of how the present cathedral was built is told in *The Accounts of the Fabric of Exeter Cathedral, 1279–1353*, ed. Audrey M. Erskine, 2 parts, Devon and Cornwall Record Society, new series 24 and 26 (1981–3). Much of the window glass is surveyed by Chris Brooks and David Evans, *The Great East Window of Exeter Cathedral: a glazing history* (Exeter, 1988). Other aspects of the cathedral's cultural history are dealt with in *Medieval Art and Architecture at Exeter Cathedral*, ed. Francis Kelly, The British Archaeological Association, Conference Transactions, 11 (1991), and in *Exeter Cathedral: a celebration*, ed. Michael Swanton (Crediton, 1991). Two pioneering studies of the cathedral close and its buildings are those of Ethel Lega-Weekes, *Some Studies in the Topography of the Cathedral Close, Exeter* (Exeter, 1915), and D. Portman, *Exeter Houses, 1400–1700* (Exeter, 1966). John Allan's article 'The College of the Vicars Choral at Exeter', in *Vicars Choral at English Cathedrals*, ed. Richard Hall and David Stocker (Oxford, 2005), is a first-rate account of that (nearly vanished) institution, and other excellent reports on parts of the cathedral and on its buildings in the close have been compiled by the staff of Exeter Archaeology. The latter may be consulted in the Cathedral Library.

The social history of the medieval cathedral, how it was used and what went on there, may be followed in Nicholas Orme, *Exeter Cathedral: As It Was 1050–1550* (Exeter, 1986). This book is being revised for republication. Kathleen Edwards's *The English Secular Cathedrals in the Middle Ages*, 2nd edn (Manchester, 1967), says much about the government of the cathedral; her account has since been extended and updated by David Lepine's *A Brotherhood of Canons Serving God: English secular cathedrals in the later middle ages* (Woodbridge, 1995), which focuses on the medieval canons. Nicholas Orme is preparing *The Minor Clergy of Exeter Cathedral: biographies, 1250–1548*, to be published by the Devon and Cornwall Record Society in 2010–11, listing and describing the medieval vicars choral, annuellars, secondaries, and choristers. David Lepine and Nicholas Orme are also the joint editors of *Death and Memory in Medieval Exeter*, Devon and Cornwall Record Society, new series 46 (2003), which covers all matters relating to the burial and commemoration of the dead in the cathedral during the middle ages.

The history of the cathedral since 1550 can be followed to some extent in general histories such as Stanford E. Lehmberg, *The Reformation of Cathedrals: cathedrals in English Society, 1485–1603* (Princeton, 1988); his *Cathedrals Under Siege: cathedrals in English society, 1600–1700* (Exeter, 1996); Owen Chadwick's *The Victorian Church*, 2 vols (London, 1966); and Philip Barrett's *Barchester: English cathedral life in the nineteenth century* (London, 1993). Much of what happened during the twentieth century is recorded in the *Friends of Exeter Cathedral Annual Reports*, beginning in 1931. Other detailed articles on various periods may be found in the two local periodicals *Devonshire Association Transactions* and *Devon and Cornwall Notes and Queries*.

NOTES

1 GOING BACK: FEBRUARY 1385

1 Nicholas Orme, *The Minor Clergy of Exeter Cathedral, 1300–1548* (Exeter, 1979), pp. 10, 56.
2 Devon Record Office, Exeter City Archives, Mayor's Court Roll 8–9 Richard II, m. 22d.
3 Exeter Cathedral Archives, D&C 2920.
4 Nicholas Orme, 'The Charnel Chapel of Exeter Cathedral', in *Medieval Art and Architecture at Exeter Cathedral*, ed. F. Kelly, The British Archaeological Association, Conference Transactions, 11 (1991), pp. 162–171.
5 Orme, *Minor Clergy*, p. 89.
6 Ibid., p. 57.
7 Ibid., pp. 22, 57.

2 THE CATHEDRAL CAT

1 J.-P. Migne, *Patrologia Cursus Completus: Series Latina* (Paris, 1844–64), vol. 150, cols. 32–3.
2 Exeter Cathedral Archives, D&C 3673, 3764–3772.
3 D&C 3766–8.

4 D&C 3768.
5 D&C 3686 fol. 47.
6 D&C 2920.
7 Ibid.
8 Exeter Cathedral Archives, Preb. V. Hope, 'An Exeter Cathedral Miscellany', p. 43.
9 Sister Seraphim, *All God's Creatures* (New York, 1966), p. 5.

3 A SPOON FOR EVERY VICAR

1 *Death and Memory in Medieval Exeter*, ed. David Lepine and Nicholas Orme, Devon and Cornwall Record Society, new series, 46 (2003), pp. 142–3. There is an earlier document similar to a will, made by Canon William de Wullaveston but it is primarily a conveyance of property (ibid., pp. 139–40).
2 Exeter Cathedral Archives, D&C ED 50. Very likely it was originally in the archives of the vicars choral, and got into private hands.
3 *Death and Memory*, ed. Lepine and Orme, pp. 150–4.
4 On the lesser cathedral clergy, see Nicholas Orme, 'The Medieval Clergy of Exeter Cathedral: I, the Vicars Choral and Annuellars', *Devonshire Association Transactions*, 113 (1981), pp. 79–102, and 'The Medieval Clergy of Exeter Cathedral: II, the Secondaries and Choristers', *Devonshire Association Transactions*, 115 (1983), pp. 79–100.

4 WHOSE BODY?

1 John Leland, *The Itinerary of John Leland*, ed. Lucy Toulmin Smith, 5 vols (London, 1907–10), i, 227.
2 *Sir George Carew's Scroll of Arms 1588*, ed. J. Brooking Rowe, *Devon Notes and Queries*, i part ii (1900–1), pp. 5, 71.

3 Sir William Pole, *Collections towards a Description of the County of Devon* (London, 1791), p. 109.

4 'A Relation of a Short Survey of the Western Counties Made by a Lieutenant of the Military Company in Norwich in 1635', ed. L. G. Wickham Legg, *Camden Miscellany XVI*, Royal Historical Society, Camden third series, 52 (1936), p. 74; R. Pearse Chope, *Early Tours in Devon and Cornwall* (Newton Abbot, 1967), p. 85.

5 Richard Symonds, *Diary of the Marches of the Royal Army during the Great Civil War*, ed. C. E. Long, Camden Society, old series, 74 (1859), p. 89.

6 Richard Polwhele, *The History of Devonshire*, 3 vols (London, 1793–1806, reprinted Dorking, 1977), ii, 15.

7 John Britton, *The History and Antiquities of the Cathedral Church of Exeter* (London, 1826), pp. 135–6.

8 George Oliver, *Monasticon Dioecesis Exoniensis* (Exeter and London, 1846), pp. 344, 346; British Library, Additional Charter 13913.

9 *The Register of Thomas de Brantyngham, Bishop of Exeter, 1370–1394*, ed. F. C. Hingeston-Randolph, 2 vols (London and Exeter, 1901–6), i, 381–2.

10 Exeter Cathedral Archives, D&C 3764.

11 *The Parliamentary Writs and Writs of Military Summons*, ed. F. Palgrave, 2 vols in 4 parts (London, Record Commission, 1827–34), i, p. 412. On the roll, its date, manuscripts, and editions, see A. R. Wagner, *A Catalogue of English Mediaeval Rolls of Arms* (London, 1950), pp. 42–50.

12 *Feudal Aids*, 6 vols (London, Public Record Office, 1899–1921), ii, 9, 38; iv, 303; v, 208.

13 *Calendar of the Register of John Drokensford, Bishop of Bath and Wells, 1309–1329*, ed. E. Hobhouse, Somerset Record Society, 1 (1887), p. 112.

14 Taunton, Somerset Record Office, Walker-Heneage and Button documents, DD\WHb/380, 773, 776–7, 779.

15 *The Accounts of the Fabric of Exeter Cathedral, 1279–1353*, ed. Audrey M. Erskine, 2 parts, Devon and Cornwall Record Society, new series, 24, 26 (1981–3), pp. 196, 198–200.

16 Nicholas Orme, 'Mortality in Fourteenth-Century Exeter', *Medical History*, 32 (1988), pp. 195–203, especially p. 199.

17 T. N. Brushfield, 'Raleghana: Part IV: Sir Henry de Ralegh, Knight, Ob. 1301', *Transactions of the Devonshire Association*, 34 (1902), pp. 455–81.

18 We possess only inadequate evidence based on sixteenth- and seventeenth-century heraldic visitations: see J. L. Vivian, *The Visitations of the County of Devon* (Exeter, 1895), p. 638.

19 On the episode, see A. G. Little and R. C. Easterling, *The Franciscans and Dominicans of Exeter*, History of Exeter Research Group, Monograph No. 3 (Exeter, 1927), pp. 40–5, 67–75.

20 Ibid., p. 44.

21 Exeter Cathedral Archives, D&C 3673, folio 88v.

22 *Calendar of Patent Rolls 1292–1301*, pp. 607, 631; *Calendar of Patent Rolls 1301–7*, pp. 8, 300, 457; *Calendar of Patent Rolls 1307–13*, pp. 23, 63; *List of Sheriffs for England and Wales . . . to A.D.1831*, Public Record Office, Lists and Indexes, 9 (London, 1898), p. 34.

23 As was noted by Brushfield, op. cit., p. 480.

24 Symonds, *Diary*, p. 92.

25 Pearse-Chope, *Early Tours in Devon and Cornwall*, p. 88.

26 Symonds, *Diary*, p. 92.

27 *The Register of Edmund Lacy: Registrum Commune*, ed. G. R. Dunstan, Devon and Cornwall Record Society, new series, 7, 10, 13, 16, 18 (1963–72), i, 99, 115, 197, 276, 285, 326; iii, 374; Exeter Cathedral Archives, D&C 764, 2395–7.

28 *Register of Lacy*, ed. Dunstan, iv, 60. On Browning, see D. Lepine, 'William Browning: A Fifteenth Century Canon of Exeter', *Friends of Exeter Cathedral, Sixty-First Annual Report* (1991), pp. 17–20.

5 ST JAMES OF EXETER

1 For Stapledon's life and death, see Mark Buck, *Politics, Finance and the Church in the Reign of Edward II. Walter Stapeldon, Treasurer of England* (Cambridge, 1983).

2 For a concise biography of James Berkeley, see the entry by the present writer in *The Oxford Dictionary of National Biography*, online version (not in the printed edition).

3 Ecclesiastes 10, verse 16.

4 For a more detailed account of Berkeley's cult, see Nicholas Orme, 'Two Saint-Bishops of Exeter', *Analecta Bollandiana*, 104 (1986), pp. 403–11.

5 J. Smyth, *The Berkeley Manuscripts. The Lives of the Berkeleys*, ed. Sir J. Maclean, 2 vols (Gloucester, 1883–6), i, 218.

6 *The Register of John de Grandisson, Bishop of Exeter*, ed. F. C. Hingeston-Randolph, 3 vols (London and Exeter, 1884–9), i, 202; ii, 941–2.

6 THE LADY OF THE SWANS

1 For Margaret's life and family, see G. E. Cokayne, *The Complete Peerage*, ed. Vicary Gibbs and others, 12 vols in 13 (London, 1910–59), iv, 324; v, 467–70.

2 On the story, see *Dictionnaire des Lettres Françaises: Le Moyen Age*, ed. Robert Bossuat and others, 2nd edn (Paris, 1994), pp. 264, 356–8, 1055, and *The Old French Crusade Cycle*, vol. i, ed. Emanuel J. Mickel and Jan A. Nelson (Alabama, 1977).

3 On the history of the swan families, see Anthony R. Wagner, 'The Swan Badge and the Swan Knight', *Archaeologia*, 97 (1959), pp. 127–38.

4 *The Complete Peerage*, vi, 463–6.

5 *The Romance of the Chevalere Assigne*, ed. H. H. Gibbs, Early English Text Society, extra series, 6 (1868).

6 John Rous, *The Rous Roll*, 2nd edn (Gloucester, 1980), p. 18.
7 *The Knight of the Swanne* (London, *c*.1560).

7 BOYS WILL BE BOYS

1 *The Old English Version of the Enlarged Rule of Chrodegang*, ed. A. S. Napier, Early English Text Society, original series, 150 (1916), pp. 53–4.
2 For more information on the choristers, see Orme, 'The Medieval Clergy of Exeter Cathedral, II: The Secondaries and Choristers', pp. 85–100, and on the development of polyphony, R. Bowers, 'To chorus from quartet: the performing resource for English Church polyphony *c*.1390–1559', in *English Choral Practice 1400–1650*, ed. J. Morehen (Cambridge, 1996), pp. 1–47.
3 *Ordinale Exon*, ed. J. N. Dalton and G. H. Doble, 4 vols, Henry Bradshaw Society, 37–8, 63, 79 (1909–40), i, 64.
4 Ibid., i, 74–7.
5 On boy-bishops, see Nicholas Orme, *Medieval Children* (London, 2001), pp. 188–9, 232–3.
6 G. Oliver, *Lives of the Bishops of Exeter and a History of the Cathedral* (Exeter, 1861), pp. 228–9.
7 Orme, *Minor Clergy*, pp. 126–32.
8 Exeter Cathedral Archives, D&C 4721/1–33.
9 D&C 3779, folios 129v, 144v.
10 Translated from Oliver, *Lives of the Bishops*, pp. 228–9. The only dating evidence relates to the clerk of the Lady chapel, whose involvement probably indicates a date after the middle of the fifteenth century.
11 A text sung on saints' days at the morning services of terce and sext and also at the morning meeting of all the clergy in the chapter-house. The reference probably means that the boys withdrew from one of these occasions at that point to have their breakfast, round about 8.00 am.

8 AN EXETER SCHOOLROOM IN THE FIFTEENTH CENTURY

1   On the history of the High School up to 1550, see Nicholas Orme, *Education in the West of England, 1066–1548* (Exeter, 1976), pp. 46–55.
2   Nicholas Orme, *Medieval Schools* (London and New Haven, 2006).
3   The school notebook is now Gonville and Caius College, Cambridge, MS 417/447; the Latin passages occur on ff 16v-24v. A good description of the book will be found in David Thomson, *A Descriptive Catalogue of Middle English Grammatical Texts* (London and New York, 1979), pp 141–7; the Latin passages are printed, translated, and discussed in Nicholas Orme, 'An English Grammar School, ca. 1450: Latin Exercises from Exeter (Caius College MS 417/447, Folios 16v–24v)', *Traditio*, 50 (1995), pp. 261–94.
4   Exeter Cathedral Archives, D&C 3551, folios 63–4.

9 WARS AND WONDERS

1   Nicholas Orme, *Exeter Cathedral: As It Was 1050–1550* (Exeter, 1986), pp. 11–12, 104. On the board-chronicle, see also pp. 75–6.
2   Exeter Cathedral Library, D&C 3508, described by N. R. Ker, *Medieval Manuscripts in British Libraries*, 4 vols (Oxford, 1969–92), ii, 814–16.
3   Folios 5r–10v.
4   Oliver, *Lives of the Bishops*, p. 333. As Ker noted, the first words of the 2nd folio in 1506, *ges terre*, match those of the surviving psalter.
5   *The Great Chronicle of London*, ed. A. H. Thomas and I. D. Thornley (London, 1938), p. 221.
6   This passage is on the April page: folio 6v.
7   Orme, 'An English Grammar School', *Traditio*, 50 (1995), pp. 261–94, especially p. 280.

8 These and other royal visits are discussed by Orme, *Exeter Cathedral: As It Was*, pp. 43–53.

9 On what follows, see Nicholas Orme, *The Cap and the Sword: Exeter and the Rebellions of 1497* (Exeter, 1997).

10 Agnes Prest is also mentioned in this book, pp. 98–9.

10 A VISITOR IN 1478

1 Corpus Christi College, Cambridge, MS 210. The parts relating to Worcester's travels have been edited as William Worcestre, *Itineraries*, ed. J. H. Harvey, Oxford, 1969, and the remainder (chiefly the description of Bristol), as William Worcestre, *The Topography of Medieval Bristol*, ed. Frances Neale, Bristol Record Society, 51 (2000).

2 For a concise biography of Worcester, see the entry by the present author in *The Oxford Dictionary of National Biography*. There are further discussions of Worcester and his work in K. B. McFarlane, *England in the Fifteenth Century* (London, 1981), pp. 199–230, and Antonia Gransden, *Historical Writing in England: II, c. 1307 to the Early Sixteenth Century* (London, 1982), pp. 308–41.

3 On Walter of Cowick, see Nicholas Orme, 'Saint Walter of Cowick', *Analecta Bollandiana*, 108 (1990), pp. 1–7.

11 THE WITCH, THE CLOCK, AND THE BISHOP

1 The Oldham chapel is mentioned in 1513 (Devon Record Office, Chanter XIII (The Register of Hugh Oldham), folio 178r. On the Speke chapel, see Nicholas Orme, 'Sir John Speke and his Chapel in Exeter Cathedral', *Devonshire Association Transactions*, 118 (1986), pp. 25–41.

2 On the cult of the Saviour in Oldham's chapel, see this book, p. 81.

3 For a concise life of Hugh Oldham, see the article by the present writer in *The Oxford Dictionary of National Biography*.

4 Orme, 'The Medieval Clergy of Exeter Cathedral: I. The Vicars and Annuellars', p. 89.

5 John Hooker alias Vowell, *A Catalog of the Bishops of Excester* (London, 1584), folio 62r; *Holinshed's Chronicles of England, Scotland and Ireland*, 6 vols (London, 1807–8), ii, 617; Devon Record Office, Exeter City Archives, Book 51, folios 336v–337r.

6 John Hooker, *The Description of the Citie of Excester*, ed. W. J. Harte and others, part ii, Devon and Cornwall Record Society (1919), p. 235.

7 It is difficult to identify this Atkins: the best candidate is Simon Atkyns, born in 1499, probably in Devon and admitted as a scholar of Corpus Christi College in 1518 (A. B. Emden, *A Biographical Register of the University of Oxford A.D. 1501 to 1540* (Oxford, 1974), pp. 16–17), but that was after Oldham had established a link with Corpus and did not concern a fellowship; the folklore may not be accurate here.

8 T. Fowler, *The History of Corpus Christi College*, Oxford Historical Society, 25 (1893), pp. 37, 60–3.

9 It seems more likely that Fox found difficulty in recruiting suitable monks from Winchester Cathedral or in providing for their needs separately from those of the other scholars.

10 Devon Record Office, Chanter XV (The Register of John Veysey, vol. ii), folio 31v.

11 Pearse Chope, *Early Tours in Devon and Cornwall*, p. 181.

12 BREAK, BREAK, BREAK

1 *Letters and Papers, Foreign and Domestic, Henry VIII*, xiii part i, pp. 79, 117, 119–20, 239.
2 *Wells Wills*, ed. F. W. Weaver (London, 1890), pp. 97–8.
3 Leland, *The Itinerary*, ed. Toulmin Smith, i, 227.
4 They are now in Exeter Museum.
5 Exeter Cathedral Archives, D&C 3552 folios 14v-15v.
6 Devon Record Office, Exeter City Archives, Book 51, folio 344r.
7 Eamon Duffy, *The Stripping of the Altars* (Cambridge, 1992), pp. 238–40.

13 TAKEN TO THE TOWER

1 For a concise account of Turberville's career, see the article by the present author in *The Oxford Dictionary of National Biography*; the article has been revised since the hard-copy dictionary appeared, and should be consulted from the online version. There is a list of Turberville's benefices in Emden, *Biographical Register of Oxford A.D. 1501 to 1540*, p. 579.
2 *The Accounts of the Wardens of the Parish of Morebath, Devon, 1520–1573*, ed. J. Erskine Binney (Exeter, 1904), p. 185; Eamon Duffy, *The Voices of Morebath* (New Haven and London, 2001), pp. 162–3.
3 John Foxe, *Acts and Monuments*, 2 vols (London, 1610), ii, 1860.
4 Hooker alias Vowell, *A Catalog of the Bishops of Excester*, sig. L folio ii verso; Exeter, Devon Record Office, Exeter City Archives, Book 51, folio 352v.
5 Foxe, *Acts and Monuments*, ii, 1859–61, 1945.
6 G. E. Phillips, *The Extinction of the Ancient Hierarchy* (London, 1905).
7 J. F. Chanter, *The Bishop's Palace, Exeter, and its Story* (London, 1932), p. 73.

14 FROM EXETER TO LONDON IN 1562

1   A brief outline of Marwood's career will be found in Emden, *Biographical Register of Oxford A.D. 1501 to 1540*, p. 385.
2   Exeter Cathedral Archives, D&C 4644.
3   Corpus Christi College, Cambridge, MS 97.
4   *The Statutes of the Realm*, vol iv part i (London, 1819), pp. 332–5.
5   C. E. Challis, *The Tudor Coinage* (Manchester, 1978), pp. 84–128.
6   London, The National Archives, PROB 11/63, folio 260r.

15 BETJEMAN AND EXETER

1   *Richard III*, Act IV scene 2.
2   Thomas Hardy, *Complete Poems*, ed. James Gibson (London, 1976), nos. 667, 669.
3   John Betjeman, *Devon: Shell Guide* (London, [1936]), pp. 24–5. The standard biography of Betjeman is by Bevis Hillier in three volumes (London, 1988–2004).
4   Exeter Cathedral Archives, Musical Lists 1935–1936.

16 AM IN ILFRACOMBE: WHY?

1   Exeter Cathedral Library, V. Hope, 'An Exeter Cathedral Miscellany', p. 27; idem, 'Exeter Cathedral Monumentarium' (1956), p. 1.
2   *The Times*, 24 June 1936, p. 18.

INDEX